BECOMING
antifragile

Becoming Antifragile: Learning to Thrive Through Disruption, Challenge and Change,
Second Edition.
Copyright © 2020, 2022 by Dr. Paige Williams.
All rights reserved.

Published by Grammar Factory Publishing, an imprint of MacMillan Company Limited.

No part of this book may be used or reproduced in any manner whatsoever without the prior written permission of the author, except in the case of brief passages quoted in a book review or article. All enquiries should be made to the author.

Grammar Factory Publishing
MacMillan Company Limited
25 Telegram Mews, 39th Floor, Suite 3906
Toronto, Ontario, Canada
M5V 3Z1

www.grammarfactory.com

Williams, Dr Paige.
Becoming Antifragile: Learning to Thrive Through Disruption, Challenge and Change / Dr Paige Williams. – Second Edition.

Paperback ISBN 978-1-98973-761-3
Hardcover ISBN 978-1-98973-763-7
eBook ISBN 978-1-98973-762-0
Audiobook ISBN 978-1-98973-768-2

1. BUS085000 BUSINESS & ECONOMICS / Organizational Behavior. 2. BUS107000 BUSINESS & ECONOMICS / Personal Success. 3. SEL024000 SELF-HELP / Self-Management / Stress Management.

Production Credits
Cover design by Designerbility
Interior layout design by Dania Zafar
Book production and editorial services by Grammar Factory Publishing

Grammar Factory's Carbon Neutral Publishing Commitment
From January 1st, 2020 onwards, Grammar Factory Publishing is proud to be neutralizing the carbon footprint of all printed copies of its authors' books printed by or ordered directly through Grammar Factory or its affiliated companies through the purchase of Gold Standard-Certified International Offsets.

Disclaimer
The material in this publication is of the nature of general comment only and does not represent professional advice. It is not intended to provide specific guidance for particular circumstances, and it should not be relied on as the basis for any decision to take action or not take action on any matter which it covers. Readers should obtain professional advice where appropriate, before making any such decision. To the maximum extent permitted by law, the author and publisher disclaim all responsibility and liability to any person, arising directly or indirectly from any person taking or not taking action based on the information in this publication.

BECOMING
antifragile

Learning to Thrive Through
Disruption, Challenge and Change

Dr PAIGE WILLIAMS

PRAISE FOR BECOMING ANTIFRAGILE

Dr Paige Williams combines intellect with insight to help us understand how to move beyond resilience to become antifragile. She gives us the science and guides us through the practices that help us both professionally and personally. This is a must read for leaders navigating complex change.

PROFESSOR LEA WATERS, PHD
ORGANISATIONAL PSYCHOLOGIST, RESEARCHER AND AUTHOR
OF THE STRENGTH SWITCH.

Never more have we needed the ability to embody the qualities of antifragile. Paige's work is a critical tool for leaders in all industries looking to build strength, longevity and a new level of adaptability in their teams. It also holds an important place at a personal level, where we all need new perspectives on how to navigate in uncertain times and reimagine a new world of work and life.

SKYE TIPLER
DIRECTOR, MKT. COMMUNICATIONS

If our life is defined by the choices we make this might be one of the most important we choose to make: to see adversity and suffering as a place for growth and opportunity. This book explores that choice brilliantly!

MATT CHURCH
LEADERSHIP EXPERT, FOUNDER, THOUGHT LEADERS

At a time when businesses – large and small – are under more pressure than ever, *Becoming Antifragile* offers leaders practical principles to help us navigate the challenges and get better from it. I found Paige's work easy to read and translate into my own leadership practice, and I've used it with my team and seen the difference it's made to their energy, attitude and mindset. This is a must read for leaders who know that there must be something beyond resilience; there is – antifragile – and this book explains how to get there.

BRIDGET BLAKE
DIRECTOR OF PARTNER ENGAGEMENT & DEVELOPMENT, SPECSAVERS ANZ

With foundations in neuroscience and psychology, *Becoming Antifragile* presents leaders with the possibility to move beyond resilience and develop the energy, attitudes and mindsets needed to meet the challenges and opportunities we are facing. The ROBUST principles provide a framework for leadership practice that can be applied across a broad range of contexts and used for personal and professional development and with teams. We are living in uncertain times; *Becoming Antifragile* is the must-have leader's guide on how to not just 'get through' them, but to come out of it better than before.

DR SARAH LEACH
GENERAL MANAGER, HEALTH, PEOPLE AND COMMUNITY, GMHBA.
ADJUNCT ASSOCIATE PROFESSOR, FACULTY OF HEALTH, DEAKIN UNIVERSITY

We already knew we were in the decade of disruption and then came the coronavirus pandemic. This may well be the system release that is needed, but how?

Dr Paige Williams has that extremely rare ability, to take big and complex ideas, like "antifragility" and not only understand them, but help you to use them in your personal and professional lives, at a time in history when we so need this. But Paige goes further, not only how to use the idea as a tool, but how to become antifragile – inspiring you to your own preparedness and potentiality. The ROBUST principles she proposes are relevant to multiple contexts in your life, at home, at work, in the best of times and the worst of times.

PROFESSOR LINDSAY OADES
DIRECTOR, CENTRE FOR POSITIVE PSYCHOLOGY, THE UNIVERSITY OF MELBOURNE.
WELLBEING PUBLIC POLICY STRATEGIST

Becoming Antifragile brings theory, research and popular culture together into an enjoyable and digestible read. Like having Paige as an executive and life coach in your ear, it's very authentic, super relevant and a real lifeline for leaders in times like this.

JENNIFER DRYSDALE
HEAD OF PHILANTHROPY, SYDNEY SYMPHONY ORCHESTRA

Deeply researched and incredibly practical, this book is an invitation for us to lead ourselves and others through disruption and uncertainty.

DR MICHELLE MCQUAID
FOUNDER AND DIRECTOR, THE MICHELLE MCQUAID COLLECTIVE

We are living in times of incredible disruption. Life as we've known it has rapidly changed. How do we manage not only our own wellbeing and productivity, but lead others through these times? The events of 2020 have revealed how fragile we have become, individually and collectively. Numerous resources point to ways to cope with, be resilient to, and manage these times of disruption. We are keeping our heads above water – barely. Could there be something more?

Becoming Antifragile offers thought-provoking, action-oriented insights of strategies for not only surviving struggle, but embracing and thriving through struggle. The book incorporates a strong empirical basis in an easy-to-read, accessible, and digestible format. The material is contextually relevant to the 21st-century workplace and the challenges and opportunities that leaders at all levels within an organisation face in their everyday lives, with examples that are relatable and inspiring.

Our workplaces are VUCA in nature, and *Becoming Antifragile* provides a refreshing, hopeful, and accessible approach for navigating the waters that we tread.

ASSOCIATE PROFESSOR PEGGY KERN, PHD
CENTRE FOR POSITIVE PSYCHOLOGY, THE UNIVERSITY OF MELBOURNE

This book is gold! If you are facing any change, uncertainty or challenge right now (and let's face it, who isn't?) then this is the book for you. It is not a book about just surviving challenging times or bouncing back. It's an insightful book which is packed full of proven and practical strategies that show us all how we can emerge from any disruption stronger, wiser and better equipped to lean into the next challenge. Read it, highlight it, revisit it, quote from it and get a copy of it into the hands of every leader you care about.

LINDA HUTCHINGS
HEAD OF FACULTY, THOUGHT LEADERS BUSINESS SCHOOL

Becoming Antifragile was thought provoking to say the least. It not only exposes some unhelpful thoughts and constructs but delivers a road map to where you would rather be. I found it inspiring, motivating and empowering.

Paige has a deep connection to her work and clearly believes that we all have the potential to thrive and to live a good life. She promotes wellness success and a win-win approach that is refreshing and speaks to a kinder, more productive world that we can all enjoy.

This book is for anyone who wants to take full responsibility for not only their life now but their legacy. The new leader will need every useful tip in this book to perform in the most disruptive decade we have ever had. Change is the only constant and *Becoming Antifragile* allows us to adjust our mindset so we can enjoy the journey while moving clearly towards the destination of our own choices.

GARRY THOMPSON
CEO, UPLIFTING AUSTRALIA

CONTENTS

Preface	1
Introduction	2
PART I: THE CASE FOR ANTIFRAGILE	**9**
1. Right Here, Right Now	11
2. Mind the Gaps	21
PART II: WHAT CAN GET YOU THERE	**33**
3. Getting to Know AntiFragile	37
4. Guiding Principles to Becoming antifragile	51
PART III: HOW TO DO IT... EVERY DAY	**103**
5. Renewable AntiFragile Energy	107
6. Courageous AntiFragile Attitudes	131
7. Infinite AntiFragile Mindsets	155
PART IV: FROM BECOMING TO BEING	**179**
8. AntiFragile Identity	181
Afterword	199
How Can I Help?	202
Let's Stay in Touch...	204

ABOUT THE AUTHOR

I am passionate about leveraging leadership capacity.

A combination of real-life leadership experience and deep academic knowledge fuels my 'superpower' of translating complex ideas and academic research to make them real, relevant, and relatable to the work that leaders do every day.

Through my conference speaking and leadership development programs I replace fear with confidence and confusion with clarity. I motivate leaders to create positive, purposeful impact for themselves and for the people they lead. I have worked with hundreds of leaders in business, government, NGOs, and education, including Specsavers, Swisse, the Magistrates Court of Victoria, the Transport Accident Commission, and the University of Melbourne.

My commercial experience is broad and deep, and my knowledge of leadership more than theoretical. Having spent more than 20 years in international leadership roles, I know what it's like to be a leader, and I have led and seen others lead both well and not so well in a wide range of contexts. This experience, supported by an undergraduate degree in business and postgraduate studies in organisational change, led to my doctoral research examining how to create positive change and wellbeing in organisations. I continue to research and teach as an Honorary Fellow of the Centre for Positive Psychology and an Associate of Melbourne Business School at The University of Melbourne.

I love to share my work. I have presented at conferences internationally and published in a range of academic and non-academic journals, including *Psychology Today* and *Human Resource Management*. I've also been interviewed for radio and a variety of podcasts, and I write a regular blog called *Leverage Points* (www.drpaigewilliams.com/leveragepoints).

As a firm believer in 'healthy body, healthy mind', I am a committed F45er and enjoy a regular yoga practice. I live on the Surf Coast of Victoria, Australia with my two adolescent daughters, who help me to keep showing up as my 'best self' every day.

I truly believe that leadership is the most potent leverage point we have to create positive change in any system, be it a family, a school, an organisation, or any team.

And I believe that each of us has a capacity for leadership that we have yet to realise. My hope is that this book helps you to realise more of yours.

With warmest wishes,

Paige

ACKNOWLEDGEMENTS

Writing does not come easily to me, and at times this book has felt like giving birth to a baby elephant! Fortunately, a number of people have helped with the 'delivery'.

To my daughters Olivia and Isabella, you are my inspiration and my motivation. Thank you for listening to my rants and dealing with my frustration as I wrestled the words out of my head and onto the pages. Thank you also for being my 'crash test dummies' and listening to me read sections aloud to make sure it made sense.

Thanks to my team – Niki Flood, my business manager; Cath Connell, my website and branding guru; and Claire Kidd, my communications expert – for keeping me on track with everything else in the world as I disappeared down the rabbit hole that was this book. Thanks to my book coach, Kelly Irving, for your advice on writing and particularly the book structure. Finally, thank you to the team at Hambone Publishing for your editing, production, and publishing expertise.

I also want to extend my thanks to a variety of people who may not even realise how much they helped me on this journey. In particular, I give my thanks to Michelle McQuaid, my friend, fellow geek, and wellbeing expert, for your support, coaching, mentoring, guidance, ideas, enthusiasm… the list goes on. And to the MMcQHQ team for their unconditional support throughout the process. To my Thought Leaders mentors Linda Hutchings and Matt Church, my friend Cynthia Mahoney, and the whole TL Tribe who make it feel like 'business as usual' to write a book a year.

Bernard de Chartres is believed to have said that we discover truths by building on previous discoveries – by 'standing on the shoulders of giants'. This book is written on the shoulders of many giants. In particular, Nassim Nicholas Taleb, who conceived the concept of anti-fragile. The world needs people like Taleb – people who challenge our paradigms and question our collective ethics. Looking in the mirror is not always pretty or comfortable, but it is very necessary. Taleb's body of work *Incerto*, of which *Antifragile* is part, forces us to do this and to be accountable for what we see.

Finally, I would like to thank my mum, who, as always, has been there as an unwavering source of love, support, and generosity, and is a living example of becoming antifragile. Thank you Mum. I love you.

PREFACE

The idea for this book was conceived in September 2019. As I started writing in January 2020 – at the beginning of what I had already begun to call the Decade of Disruption – I could not have foreseen the events that would unfold in the coming months.

The global COVID-19 pandemic changed patterns of working and living across the globe in just a few short weeks. With a level of disruption not experienced at this scale since the world wars or the Great Depression, it will undoubtedly leave an indelible mark on world history.

This book was not written in response to COVID-19. The ideas within were conceived and collated well before the pandemic took hold. Nevertheless, it is a timely context that lays bare the fragility of our modern world and the processes, structures, and dynamics that create it. The case for becoming antifragile was present before COVID-19. But in the wake of COVID-19 it is more compelling than ever.

At a time when disruption, uncertainty, and challenge are amplified to extraordinary levels, I believe that understanding how to become antifragile will help us answer the question 'How can we be better from this experience?' with honesty and humility. And I believe that by becoming antifragile, we can take effective action that makes a difference in our own lives and in the world at large.

INTRODUCTION

> *As our expectations drift further and further from our reality, we have become less able to cope than ever before. We feel fragile.*

WHEN SOMETHING IS FRAGILE, IT BREAKS easily – a window pane, a crystal glass, your mother's antique vase. These things require careful handling because they don't perform well under stress and pressure. When we are dealing with something fragile, we handle it carefully and make exceptions to accommodate its delicate nature.

The same is true of people. When we are feeling fragile, our world becomes smaller. We feel less able to deal with the challenges and engage with the opportunities of life. We're just getting through.

So what is the opposite of fragile?

Words like *strong*, *robust*, *sturdy*, and *resilient* come to mind. And yet these don't capture the true opposite of fragile. If fragile is broken, overwhelmed, crushed, or defeated by adverse conditions, then the opposite would grow, develop, and improve in that same type of environment.

> *The opposite of fragile thrives through disruption, challenge, and change.*
>
> *The opposite of fragile is antifragile.*

The word *antifragile* was coined by Nassim Nicholas Taleb in his 2011 book *Antifragile: Things That Gain Through Disorder*. Taleb uses it in the context of socioeconomic and political systems and their ability to withstand disruption and unpredictable events.

INTRODUCTION

When something is fragile, shock or disorder hurts and perhaps even breaks it. When it is robust and resilient, it can withstand shocks and disorder and even bounce back from them. But what if we take it one step further? When something is truly antifragile, it *improves* through uncertainty, shock, and disorder; it *improves* through the experiences of uncertainty, challenge, and change that come with disruption.

When we are antifragile we improve through stress, pressure, and adversity.

I've often wondered, how is it that some people, teams, and organisations are able to 'read the landscape' – almost as if they have a crystal ball – and elegantly adjust by reinventing themselves, innovating new ideas, and meeting new market needs? When life happens and things tip on their head – a merger, a restructure, a new CEO, a new project – how is it that some leaders are able to navigate the struggle and challenge, whilst others just spin their wheels, devolving into pointless circles or collapsing under the pressure?

Like you, in my professional and personal life I've experienced ups and downs, challenges and opportunities, joy and sadness. Some of these I handled better than others, some I survived more intact than others, and some helped me learn and grow in ways that enabled me to thrive.

Why?

I first came across the word *antifragile* in Mark Manson's *Everything is F*cked: A Book About Hope*. Working from the basis that pain is a universal constant, Manson suggests that everything we do, are, and care about reflects our choice to be fragile or antifragile. This captured my attention. What would it mean for a person to 'become antifragile'? How could we develop antifragile human systems?

With these questions burning in my head, I read Taleb's original work. In it, Taleb challenges our current operating model of capitalism, questions our slavish admiration of academia and 'empty experts', and supports the value of the collective over individualism. At the same time, he warns of the 'bigger is better' mentality that dominates our current political and economic systems and exposes the fragility inherent in the complexity and hyper-connectedness of centralised government and massive global corporations.

But it was the principles that underpinned Taleb's work that interested me. What could antifragile look like for individuals? How could these principles help leaders become antifragile, and even go beyond that to support antifragile teams, cultures, organisations…?

ANTIFRAGILE LEADERS

Through my 20+ years of experience as a business leader, my doctoral research, and my professional work with hundreds of leaders across business, government, NGOs, and education, I see that leaders need help to:

- move beyond just 'getting through'
- experience gain rather than loss from disruption, challenge, and change
- understand how we are making ourselves fragile and what will help us become antifragile.

The ideas and possibilities exploded! The idea of *antifragility* appealed to me as much in the context of my own lived experience as from a theoretical and academic perspective. It provided a different view on many of the challenges I had faced as a leader and drew together the fields of academic work I had been playing in for over 10 years. Here was something I had experienced in both my personal and my professional life, over and over again. Here was something I could help people understand, learn, and live, and in doing so provide immense value – for them, and also for me. For the first time in my life, I felt a sense of my work as a calling.

This was a book I felt compelled to write.

INTRODUCTION

ABOUT THIS BOOK...

I like to have things to look forward to and to know where I'm going, so let me start with a primer on what's ahead for you.

In Part I we examine the case for becoming antifragile by exploring what makes us fragile, and the implications this has for us as leaders. We answer the question *Why do I need to go on this journey?*

In Part II we get to know the antifragile landscape better by exploring what it is and isn't, before unfolding our map for the Becoming Antifragile journey.

Once we've scoped the landscape and understood the map, our journey will progress in four stages. In Part II, we focus on the first two stages: locating your position, and becoming familiar with a 'Travel Guide' of principles to guide your journey.

1. Locate your position

Before you can embark on a journey, you need to know your starting point. You can work out your precise position on the map by taking the antifragile survey and getting a personalised report at www.theantifragilesurvey.com. If you're not one for surveys, that's fine! You'll be invited to get a gauge on your location by considering a few simple questions along the way.

2. Get the Travel Guide

In Chapter 4 we apply Taleb's principles for antifragile sociopolitical and economic systems to a system of one: you. Like a Lonely Planet Guide for becoming antifragile, the ROBUST principles will help you navigate your journey without simply telling you where to go. These principles are designed to be easily applied to your everyday life and work as a leader.

In Part III, we get into the nitty gritty of the actual route you'll take to become antifragile.

3. Plan your route

Becoming antifragile is a unique journey for each of us, and that means we each need a personalised route plan. In Part III we look at what it means to have Antifragile Energy, Antifragile Attitudes, and Antifragile Mindsets. We explore how applying the ROBUST principles to these three things can help you reduce fragility, build robustness, and make a difference in your life and leadering. By the end of this section, you'll understand what the first steps of your Becoming Antifragile journey could look like.

4. Take your first steps… and keep going!

Map? Check.
Travel Guide? Check.
Personalised route plan? Check.
Time to get going!

Sounds easy, right? But sometimes it *isn't* that easy, and even once you get started, it can be really hard to keep going. So in Part IV we'll look at what it means to move from *becoming* to *being* antifragile and how, by using the latest research on behaviour change, you can create helpful habits that keep you moving rather than anchoring you in place.

Along the way you'll meet Alex – an up-and-coming leader facing many of the challenges that I've seen and experienced – and join Alex's journey to becoming antifragile. You'll also meet other people in Alex's life and see how they experience fragility and antifragility and what impact that has.

Summaries at the end of each chapter make it easy to review or preview content. Parts II and III also feature easy-to-use summaries of all the actions suggested throughout the chapters as a practical checklist.

One more note: you'll notice I use the word *leadering* rather than *leadership* throughout the book – a verb, rather than a noun. This is not a grammatical error. Rather, it is a way to communicate my belief that leadering is *active*, and intentional. It is something we do every day, and it is available to everyone. As distinct from the action of leading, leadering is about *being* a leader – of yourself and of others. It's about how we show up in the world and the impact that has. It's the 'little-l' leadership you show every day.

Leadering happens. Everyone does it. We get to choose *how*. By the end of this book, you will understand why antifragile leadering always wins out, and you will be ready to apply it in your own life.

MY INVITATION TO YOU

Courage and comfort are a bit like Apple and Microsoft – rarely seen together! But having the courage to sit with, engage, and lean into the discomfort that comes with uncertainty and disruption is the essence of Becoming AntiFragile.

> *Take the path of courage as you read this book.*
> *Take a bigger, braver view on the impact you could have in your world and the world at large.*

To take on board the ideas I share with you here – to really absorb them into your identity – may mean making deep changes to your beliefs, to the stories you tell yourself about who you are and how you lead. It will mean taking a real, honest look in the mirror at how you show up, what is serving you, and how you may be helping or hindering yourself and those around you. And it will ask you to take a bigger, braver view on the impact you could have in your world and the world at large if you embrace the courage to show up, to take risks and learn from them, and to choose to intentionally lead *your* life, *your* way.

I invite you to take the path of courage as you read this book. To let go of your current ways of thinking and behaving when they do not serve you; to embrace the opportunity to lean into challenge rather than avoid it; to embrace uncertainty and to learn to thrive through disruption and change. I invite you to achieve things through your leading, for yourself and for others, that you had never imagined possible. In becoming antifragile, I hope that you become more of who you truly are and experience more of what you truly want.

Let's begin.

PART I

THE CASE FOR ANTIFRAGILE

'Really, Paige? Do I need to become antifragile? I've got a lot going on right now...'

I hear you!

If you're going to invest your time and effort, you need to know that becoming antifragile will actually bring results. So in this section we'll examine the case for becoming antifragile through two timeframes – what's going on right now, and what we've got to look forward to.

As we begin a new decade, our environment is becoming more complex, more uncertain, and more affected by 'wicked problems' than ever before.

Climate change, scarcity of resources, and the rise of nationalism in global political and economic dynamics are having widespread impacts on the way we live and relate to each other. At the same time, the so-called Fourth Industrial Revolution has brought a new complexity to the workplace, with the opportunities of artificial intelligence and an increasingly diverse workforce who often work remotely. And in our personal lives, we are experiencing and responding to changing family structures, more working parents, an ageing population, and technology that allows us to be constantly connected – often in all the wrong ways. In this context, resilience is no longer enough. Welcome to the Decade of Disruption.

Resilience is no longer enough in the Decade of Disruption.

Add to this the impact of COVID-19 and now more than ever, we need to understand how to thrive through this disruption, challenge, and change. We need to let go of old ways of being, doing, and leading based on the belief that we can control and predict what's coming. We need to accept the inevitability of change, stop fighting it, and use it to leverage opportunity, growth, and development by asking, *How can we be better coming out of this than we were coming in?*

The thinking that got us here isn't going to see us through what lies ahead. We need to embrace the unknown, the uncertain, the unexpected, the unplanned, and the unwanted that life throws at us. We need to start becoming antifragile.

1.

RIGHT HERE, RIGHT NOW

IN NOVEMBER 2019, A 55-YEAR-OLD MAN FROM HUBEI PROVINCE in China contracted a pneumonia virus of unknown origin. By the end of June 2020, over 10 million people in more than 200 countries and territories around the world had contracted what was now known as COVID-19. Over 510,000 people had died, and experts estimated that it would be 12–18 months before a vaccine was available to the public.

Almost overnight, non-essential businesses around the globe shut down; office workers were sent to work from home; schools closed. Many countries imposed quarantines or entry bans for citizens and visitors, and some set up border controls. International and domestic travel was severely restricted.

People were told to stay indoors and to leave their homes only for essentials – work, food, medical attention, and one period of exercise per day. In Australia, people were asked to keep a physical distance of 1.5 metres from others whenever they were outside the home in order to help prevent the virus from spreading, and supermarkets and stores put markers on the ground to reinforce this measure. Worldwide, 2.6 billion people – around a third of the global population and more than were alive in World War II – were under some form of lockdown.

People panicked. Supermarkets ran out of stock; shelves emptied; people fought over toilet paper. Purchase quantities were restricted for in-demand items. Hand sanitiser and face masks became as coveted as diamonds.

As for the economic impact, it was nothing short of devastating. In the week ending 28 February 2020, stock markets worldwide saw their largest single-week declines since the 2008 global financial crisis. Global stock markets crashed even further in March 2020, with falls of several percent in the world's major indices.

As the pandemic continued to spread, global conferences and events across industries as diverse as technology, fashion, and sports were cancelled or postponed. Production of film and television programs was shut down or delayed, Disney closed its parks across the globe, and Pope Francis livestreamed the Holy Week liturgies from St. Peter's Basilica in Rome. There was not a single industry sector that wasn't impacted in some way as governments were forced to prepare and implement massive bailout packages.

It was history in the making.

Whilst the impact on the global economy is yet to be fully realised, at the time of writing, it is estimated to be in the trillions and anticipated to change the face of world politics forever. International Monetary Fund (IMF) managing director Kristalina Georgieva declared that the global economy will contract in 2020, and that this 'recession [is] at least as bad as during the global financial crisis or worse.' By June 2020 the IMF was deploying its entire lending capacity of 1 trillion USD to meet requests for support from over 100 member countries. This was a 'black swan' of epic proportions, and it showed just how fragile we had become.

DANGER! BLACK SWANS AHEAD

The term 'black swan' is used in economics to describe a high-profile, hard-to-predict, and rare event that is beyond the realm of normal expectations in history, science, finance, and technology based on past experience. 'Black swan theory' was developed by Nassim Nicholas Taleb in his book *Black Swans: The Impact of the Highly Improbable*. Taleb suggests that black swans have three attributes: 'First, it is an outlier, as it lies outside the realm of regular expectations, because nothing in the past can convincingly point to its possibility. Second, it carries an extreme "impact". Third, in spite of its outlier status, human nature makes us concoct explanations for its occurrence after the fact, making it explainable and predictable.' So significant are the repercussions of black swan events that a small number explain almost everything in our world, from the success of ideas and religions, to the dynamics of historical events, to the trajectories of our own personal lives.

Black swan events are rare, have extreme impact, and are 'predictable' only in retrospect.

Whilst the debate about whether COVID-19 was a 'true' black swan continues, the learning we can take from black swan theory is that we need to be prepared for what we cannot predict. We cannot predict every disruption in our lives, nor the uncertainty, challenge, or change they may bring. But whether it is a promotion or a redundancy, a new job or a new boss, the start of a new relationship or the end of a current one, we can 'be better' from our experiences. And becoming antifragile helps us to do just that.

WE MAKE OURSELVES FRAGILE

Unfortunately, many of the habits, systems, processes, and mindsets that characterise our modern society contribute to making us fragile. We are so obsessed with being 'right', being 'successful', and being 'perfect' that we try to remove any and all stressors from our lives. The problem is, without challenges and volatility, we become weaker. And when the inevitable failures, falls, and obstacles do happen, we don't have the skills or resources to cope.

The hyper-connectivity provided by social media is leading many of us to rest too much of our self-identity, self-concept, and self-belief in the hands of others. All too often the way we feel about ourselves comes down to how many 'likes' or comments our latest story received. Just as hyper-connectivity can make an economic system fragile to disruption (just look at the impact of COVID-19), social hyper-connectivity can do the same thing to individuals.

As leaders, there are certain practices that make us and our teams more fragile. In particular, we make ourselves and our teams more fragile when we fail to recognise our biases and 'default' thinking patterns. When we continually listen to the same voices with similar perspectives to our own (the 'echo chamber') rather than seeking diversity and supporting healthy conflict. When we fall into the trap of expecting that systems and processes will 'take care of things' instead of doing the real work that needs to be done. When we put off the uncomfortable conversation with *that* team member until the next performance review cycle instead of addressing the issues now, while they are current and relevant. Any time we avoid the stress and challenge of discomfort, we make ourselves – and our teams – weaker and more fragile.

We make ourselves weaker when we overprotect and avoid stress and challenge.

Another common problem is that we tend to underestimate randomness. Think about the people in your team or your family – the variety of ages, backgrounds, knowledge and skill levels, and personality types. It's a firework of randomness just waiting to ignite! So why do we downplay its impact? Our minds can play tricks on us through our cognitive biases and selective memory, turning history into a smooth, linear timeline that simply doesn't reflect reality. As a result, we have a tendency to focus on 'typical' situations rather than understanding and accounting for the fact that we exist within complex systems, with interdependencies that can be hard to detect and responses that are hard to predict. Then when something unexpected does happen, we overreact and can't cope.

Have you ever learned something valuable from getting it wrong? When you look back at your most important lessons in life, have some (perhaps most?) come from times when you were challenged? When you were really pushed to your limits? Yup, me too.

There's little doubt – and lots of evidence – that we learn more from our mistakes and failures than from our successes. Personal disruption leads to growth. And that's because complex systems – like human beings – need challenge and stress to thrive.

Research by The Wellbeing Lab found that thriving and struggle often go hand in hand. The results suggest that Australian workers who self-reported as 'living well despite struggles' performed just as well as those who felt they were 'consistently thriving'. They also had similar (and higher) levels of job satisfaction and commitment to their organisation than workers who were 'just getting by' or 'really struggling'. This is backed up by research by Dr Adam Fraser with 800 professionals working in highly complex and changing environments. Fraser found that if we see struggle as a threat, because we fear we might make a mistake, fail, or be exposed as incompetent, we focus on trying to avoid struggle or blame others. In contrast, when we see struggle as a challenge and focus on the growth opportunities it offers, we are more likely to strive, evolve, and be innovative. Fraser suggests that striving through struggle enables us to tolerate being uncomfortable whilst focusing on the growth that will come from our experiences.

The truth is, when we avoid small mistakes, it makes the impact and fallout of the big ones more severe. By introducing smaller doses of stress, disruption, and challenge, we make the system (that's you!) as a whole stronger and more able to deal with larger doses, to the extent that it actually develops and improves through the experience.

In the volatile, uncertain context of the Decade of Disruption, it is better to create an antifragile system that learns and grows through trial and error than to play it safe and try to be right all the time. Why? Because prediction in the Decade of Disruption is impossible. Unexpected

The essence of becoming antifragile is being prepared for what we can't predict.

events are inevitable, and we can only respond effectively – and perhaps come out stronger for it – if we are antifragile. In fact, this is the very essence of becoming antifragile: being prepared for what we can't predict. And this means lassoing the black swan around the neck, hanging on tight, and maybe even enjoying the ride!

SUMMARY

- *The COVID-19 pandemic has exposed how fragile we have become.*
- *We rely too much on external factors, avoid discomfort, and underestimate randomness.*
- *The habits, systems, and processes of our modern world contribute to our fragility; we demonise failure and are in constant pursuit of perfection.*
- *Research shows that when we see struggle as a challenge and focus on what we can learn from it, we are better equipped to thrive.*
- *Smaller doses of stress, disruption, and challenge make the bigger issues more manageable so that we can evolve through them.*
- *In the complex, interconnected world we now live in, we need to be prepared for what we can't predict. We need to become antifragile.*

REFERENCES

By the start of April 2020, over 1.1 million people... World Health Organization (WHO) (2020, January 20). Q&A on coronaviruses (COVID-19)". Retrieved 11 March 2020. Johns Hopkins CSSE. Coronavirus COVID-19 Global Cases by the Center for Systems Science and Engineering (CSSE) at Johns Hopkins University (JHU). ArcGIS. Johns Hopkins CSSE. Retrieved 11 April 2020. Hui, D. S., Azhar, E. I., Madani, T. A., Ntoumi, F., Kock, R., Dar, O., et al. (February 2020). The continuing 2019-nCoV epidemic threat of novel coronaviruses to global health—The latest 2019 novel coronavirus outbreak in Wuhan, China. *Int J Infect Dis.* 91: 264–66. doi:10.1016/j.ijid.2020.01.009

Whilst the impact on the global economy is yet to be fully realised... https://www.afr.com/policy/economy/imf-forecasts-2020-global-recession-recovery-in-2021-20200324-p54d7h

By the end of March, 2.6 billion people worldwide – around a third of the world's population and more than were alive in World War II – were under some form of lockdown... https://www.sciencealert.com/one-third-of-the-world-s-population-are-now-restricted-in-where-they-can-go

"First, it is an outlier, as it lies outside the realm of regular expectations, because nothing in the past can convincingly point to its possibility. Second, it carries an extreme 'impact'. Third, in spite of its outlier status, human nature makes us concoct explanations for its occurrence after the fact, making it explainable and predictable." Taleb, Nassim Nicholas (2010) [2007]. *The Black Swan: The Impact of the Highly Improbable* (2nd ed.). London: Penguin. ISBN 978-0-14103459-1.

There's little doubt – and lots of evidence... Medlock L. S. (2014, April 11). Don't fear failure: Nine powerful lessons we can learn from our mistakes. https://www.huffingtonpost.com/lisabeth-saunders-medlock-phd/dont-fear-failure-9-powerful-lessons-we-can-learn-from-our-mistakes_b_6058380.html

Research by the Wellbeing Lab found that... The Wellbeing Lab 2020 Workplace Survey. https://www.michellemcquaid.com/product/wlab-2020-workplace-survey/

This is backed up by research conducted by Dr Adam Fraser which shows that... Fraser, Adam (2020). Strive, Embracing the Gift of Struggle. Milton: Wiley. ISBN: 9780730337416

MEET ALEX

It was Monday morning and Alex had just made it to work – later than planned, again. Even now, juggling a takeaway coffee (aka breakfast) in one hand and a weekend's worth of files in the other, the office was a welcome retreat from the chaos of the 'morning routine'.

With three children under 15 and a partner with a small business, to say that Alex's mornings were busy would be an understatement. Packed lunches, excursion forms, after-school- activity transport negotiations, the usual breakfast and missing school uniform issues (the washing machine must eat socks!)… the list went on! This morning the added call from Mum about Dad's chest infection had meant it was a miracle only 20 minutes had been lost from the start of the day. Unfortunately, that had eaten up most of Alex's prep time for the morning's team meeting.

With 10 minutes to go until the meeting, Alex hastily jotted down some agenda items whilst thinking of the recent conversation with the Operations Director, Glenn. The project was behind schedule, the budget had been blown, and the overseas client wasn't happy – in fact, they'd started to raise questions about the team's capacity to deliver.

The truth was, there were a few team members who tended to sit back without offering ideas, didn't help to move things forward, and always seemed to come up with reasons why not rather than ask, 'How could we…?' It was draining trying to motivate and energise them, especially when they were spread across different states, countries, and time zones. To make matters even worse, the project brief and scope kept moving as the client reacted to changes in their customer market.

Alex couldn't help but wonder: *Does it have to be like this? What am I doing wrong? Is there another way?*

Snapping back to reality, Alex focused again on the scribbled agenda.

Pushing down rising feelings of overwhelm at the looming project deadlines, Alex walked into the meeting, thinking, *Let's just get through this...*

WHAT DO YOU SEE?

- In what ways is Alex struggling?
- What is making Alex fragile?
- Do you recognise any of these factors in your own life?

2.
MIND THE GAPS

THE CONSEQUENCES OF ADVANCEMENT AND PROGRESS IN THE physical world – information overload, isolation, and breakdown of social systems – have outstripped our psychological developmental capacity. And the gap between what philosopher Ken Wilber calls our 'internal and external worlds' is getting bigger. Whilst biologically and physiologically we may be adapting and evolving to the needs and demands of our context, psychologically we are not keeping up. We simply cannot cope with the world we have created.

> *We cannot cope with the complex world we have created.*

For many of us, the world is becoming more uncertain and open to disruption. The level, pace, and complexity of change is increasing, and technology is advancing in ways most of us can only imagine. Scarcity of resources, increasing nationalism, and a growing divide between rich and poor have created volatile environments throughout history, and this volatility is only increasing with the impact of COVID-19.

The term VUCA – volatile, uncertain, complex, and ambiguous – was once reserved for military contexts, but now applies to our everyday personal and professional lives. It is perhaps the only constant as technology opens up the world to us and we experience more of it. Has the world itself become more VUCA? Maybe, maybe not, but we are certainly more exposed to information that makes it *feel* like it is. Where once we were drinking from a water fountain, we're now trying to drink from a fire hydrant. And our brains are drowning.

> Our brains are drowning in the quantity and nature of information we are exposed to.

In this context it is hardly surprising to see an epidemic of anxiety and stress sweeping across all layers and levels of the population. Depression is currently the most common mental health issue on the planet, with nearly 300 million people affected around the world. The World Health Organization expects that by 2030 depression will have become the largest single healthcare burden, costing $6 trillion per year globally.

Research by mental health support service Beyond Blue suggests that one-quarter of Australians will experience an anxiety condition in their lifetime, that one in six has experienced anxiety or depression in the last 12 months, and that one in seven is *currently* experiencing an anxiety condition. Suicide is the leading cause of death among young Australians. About 350 young people aged 15–24 take their own lives every year – more than die in road accidents. For every youth suicide, there are up to 200 more attempts. People of all ages, races, genders, incomes, and family backgrounds commit suicide, but young people are especially at risk.

I see three main 'gaps' that expose our fragility and will only get bigger in the future. They are:

- Safety versus risk
- Expectations versus reality
- Stability versus disruption

GAP 1: SAFETY VERSUS RISK

When it comes to our ancestral gene pool, it was 'survival of the safest' rather than 'survival of the fittest' that won the day. When we were

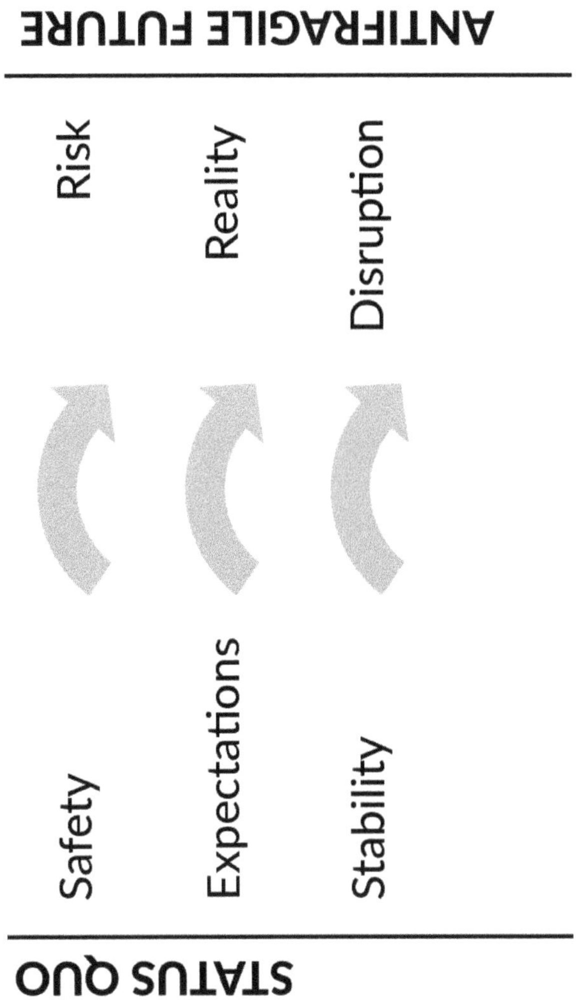

ANTIFRAGILE FUTURE

Risk

Reality

Disruption

Safety

Expectations

Stability

STATUS QUO

Figure 2.1: The fragility gaps

living on the plains of Africa, was it the gene of courage, prompting us to stay and fight the tiger, that supported survival? Nope! No heroes required here, thanks. It was the gene that helped us to sense danger and compelled us to run first or fastest that guaranteed we got to hunt for another dinner rather than become one. So the gene pool from which we are derived comes from the 'safest of the safe' brains, because that's what kept us alive and helped the tribe survive.

But when it comes to disrupted, uncertain, volatile environments, playing it safe just isn't the best option. Playing it safe assumes that we can control our context, that we can predict or model what the possible outcomes could be, that planned strategic action will see us through. But in the complex, uncertain world we've created, that isn't enough. We need to take intelligent risks in order to meet the challenges and benefit from the opportunities that the Decade of Disruption will inevitably provide.

GAP 2: EXPECTATIONS VERSUS REALITY

Much of the fragility we create and the pain we suffer comes from the gap between our expectations – what we believe the world 'should' look like – and what we actually experience day to day. We see this in all areas of life.

What are our expectations of leaders?

As I work with my clients, a common theme I hear is that they are expected to do more with less. Shorter deadlines mean less time, streamlined teams mean fewer people, and budget constraints mean fewer resources. It can feel like a no-win situation, and that leaves leaders feeling helpless and hopeless. What 'should' leaders do?

What are our expectations of business?

As the debate around our role in the health of the planet intensifies, traditional models of business and economics based on Milton Friedman's 'shareholder theory', which holds that a business' primary responsibility is to its shareholders, are being challenged. Models that recognise the role of business in advancing meaningful progress and contributing to the greater good of the world are gaining support, particularly from millennials. What 'should' the role of business be?

What are our expectations of life?

'Life satisfaction' measures how people evaluate their life as a whole, as distinct from what they may be feeling right now. It is what's called a 'global evaluation', as opposed to a specific one. We can experience satisfaction in different areas of life, including work, relationships, family and friends, personal development, and health and fitness. A person feels 'life satisfaction' when they judge that their real life reflects or fulfils their ideal life plan. And this is the issue.

Our expectations of what an 'ideal life plan' looks like have become unrealistic. The expectations we have of ourselves, our achievements, our relationships with loved ones, the fulfilment we get from work, our physical health and appearance, and our love life create a constant sense of disappointment and dissatisfaction when they are not met. We see other people's 'perfect' personal lives on social media and their 'perfect' professional lives on LinkedIn and we assume we are falling behind. In reality we are only seeing what others want to us to see and not the complete picture. On a cognitive level most of us realise this, but we still can't help but compare ourselves to these unrealistic, 'untrue' standards and then berate ourselves when we don't come close. We have created our own echo chamber, and we don't like how it sounds. What 'should' our lives comprise?

GAP 3: STABILITY VERSUS DISRUPTION

In a VUCA world, traditional approaches to leadership, strategy, and change just don't work. The dominant leadership narrative in most workplaces assumes a system that is mostly stable and that simply requires data, analysis, leadership visions, and plans to solve problems and to realise opportunities that arise. Unfortunately, because we can't model the future based solely on the past, these leadership visions often turn out to be wrong – and even when they are right, we don't realise quickly enough because the feedback lag time is too long. In a rapidly changing and diverse world, traditional approaches to leadership are not only ineffective, they actually create barriers to success.

On a global scale, prevailing economic dynamics have changed little since the end of World War II in 1945. For example, although the United States has established itself as a world state, its overly complex and densely connected resources and power structures, levels of bureaucracy, and layers of administration have stifled innovation. As a result, systems have failed to adapt to the changes around them.

When systems remain stable rather than responsive to changes in their context like this, they become stagnant and fragile. We can see the effects of this systemic inflexibility at many levels. Here are just a few that are being lived out in many nations – including Australia – across the world:

- Mental health issues rise as people are unable to access the support they need to close the gap between their internal and external worlds.

- Consumer debt levels are higher than at any point in history as we try to buy our way out of the gap between expectations and reality.

- New business creation is stagnant as we demonise failure, quash innovation, and create financial systems that disadvantage start-ups.

- Wealth disparity has grown to epic proportions. In 2020, the 20 richest people in the world are worth the same as the bottom 50% (that's 3.75 billion people).

- Political polarisation continues to spread across the globe as leaders with narrow agendas and short-term perspectives gain power.

- Shared cultural values within and across nations are increasingly fragmented as we become focused on 'saving ourselves'.

We need a 'system release' that clears the way for innovation and increases capacity to deal with future shocks and change.

What these systems need is 'system release' – a phase of reorganisation that clears the way for innovation and increases the system's capacity to deal with future shocks and change. Only then can a system become antifragile.

As we entered the Decade of Disruption, and even before the impact of COVID-19, this system release was already long overdue. In a context of rapidly advancing technology and increasing globalisation, our fragile systems had created an environment in which disruption was inevitable. And as we scramble to catch up with the scale and pace of change that results from our 'advancement', VUCA is the new normal.

HOW CAN WE CLOSE THE GAPS?

We simply cannot prevent, predict, or control the disruption, challenge, and change inherent in the VUCA environment we have created. Although research suggests we are born with an inherent level of resilience, we are making ourselves fragile through the world we have created and the expectations we hold. As the gap between our expectations and the current reality gets bigger, many of us are falling into the danger zone for anxiety and depression. On a day-to-day basis, for most of us, robustness is no longer a part of who we are.

Like a lizard losing its tail, we need a mechanism by which the system – us – regenerates itself continuously by *using* rather than *suffering* from unpredictable events, shocks, stressors, and volatility. This is what becoming antifragile is all about.

In Becoming Antifragile we use rather than suffer from unpredictable events, stressors, and uncertainty, and in doing so, we prepare ourselves to face what we can't predict.

It allows us to deal with the unknown, to do things without necessarily understanding them, and to do them well. It prepares us to face what we can't predict, and to lean into disruption, challenge, and change. It is how we learn to thrive in the Decade of Disruption.

SUMMARY

» *The volatile, uncertain, complex, and ambiguous (VUCA) environment we now live in has resulted in increased stress, anxiety, depression, and other mental health issues.*

» *Our fragility is centred around three main gaps:*

   1. *Safety vs risk – our ancestral 'survival of the safest' instinct no longer serves us.*

   2. *Expectation vs reality – we don't live the lives we feel we 'should' be living.*

   3. *Stability vs disruption – our embedded systems leave no opportunity for innovation and growth.*

» *To become antifragile, systems – including us – need a 'release' that allows them to reorganise and to clear the way for innovation and increase capacity to deal with future shocks and change.*

» *To do this we need a mechanism by which the system regenerates itself continuously by **using** rather than **suffering** from unpredictable events.*

REFERENCES

And the gap between what philosopher Ken Wilber calls... Wilber, Ken (2018) [2007]. The Integral Vision. Boston: Shambhala ISBN: 9781611806427

Suicide is the leading cause of death among young Australians... https://www.healthdirect.gov.au/youth-suicide

Depression is currently the most common mental health issue on the planet, with 300 million people affected around the world... https://www.who.int/mental_health/in_the_workplace/en/

The World Health Organization expects that by 2030 depression will have become the largest single healthcare burden, costing $6 trillion per year globally.... https://www.blackdoginstitute.org.au/news/news-detail/2018/03/05/technology-and-the-future-of-mental-health

Research by mental health support service Beyond Blue... https://www.beyondblue.org.au/media/statistics

Wealth disparity of epic proportions... https://www.forbes.com/billionaires/ https://www.youtube.com/watch?v=NEnuWv38url

Although research suggests we are born with an inherent level of resilience... Bonanno, G. (2019). The Other Side of Sadness: What the New Science of Bereavement Tells Us About Life After Loss. New York: NY. Basic Books.

A RISING STAR

Alex's boss Glenn gaped at the number of unread emails in her inbox. *Really?* she thought to herself. *How can that many have come in over the last 24 hours? I spent an hour clearing them on Saturday evening – making me late for dinner. Not sure the effort was worth the trouble I got in for it!*

Glenn noticed that several of the emails were from the same client – Alex's big project. Hmm, Alex… definitely a rising star, lots of potential, but also heading for burnout. Glenn thought back over their recent conversation. Alex wanted to please everyone – the client, the team, Glenn – and was always trying to provide all the answers. Doing more and fixing things was clearly the pattern of working that got Alex promoted, but it wasn't the right approach at this level. The project team was diverse in terms of personality, experience, and geographic locations; Glenn knew there were complexities. But Alex relied too much on the opinions of a few members of the team and wasn't prepared to challenge them, to take a risk.

Glenn could see that the team dynamics were stale – similar ways of thinking, not much creativity or innovation. What they needed, she thought, was for some new people to come in to help them think about the issues in new ways and from different perspectives. Glenn had brought this up in her meeting with Alex, suggesting a few 'guest attendees' at team meetings to mix things up over the next few weeks, but Alex seemed reluctant, saying something about not being sure 'how the team would take it'. That was another issue – Alex was too concerned about the team's personal opinions. Sometimes people needed to experience and live through the 'pain' of challenge to get to where they needed to be, Glenn thought. She was meeting with Alex again today, so she'd check in again then. In the meantime, back to tackling the inbox.

WHAT DO YOU SEE?

- Based on Glenn's reflections above, what is Alex doing that increases fragility?
- Where are the 'fragility gaps' in the scenario above?
- Which of the three fragility gaps are impacting your own life and leadering?

PART II

WHAT CAN GET YOU THERE

Now that you understand the case for becoming antifragile, in this section we'll explore the antifragile landscape more closely, unfold the map for your Becoming Antifragile journey, and locate your position on the map (www.theantifragilesurvey.com). We'll also dive into the ROBUST principles that will act as our Antifragile Travel Guide, helping us to navigate the landscape like a local.

Antifragility underpins everything that changes over time. Just consider evolution, culture, ideas, innovation, even us as a species. These complex, organic, 'living' systems improve through disruption and change – they adapt to make the most of their new conditions. In contrast, static, inert systems are slow and inactive. They cannot or do not adapt, and so they collapse or break under the pressure of disruption and change. They are fragile.

Whether we are fragile or robust, resilient or antifragile reflects how we feel about the relative balance between the levels of disruption, challenge, and change in our environment, and our resources and capacity to respond to it. The larger the gap between what is being asked of us and what we have to give, the more fragile we are likely to feel. In Chapter 3 we unpack a more nuanced understanding of what antifragile is to better understand the landscape and open up the map that will guide us on our journey.

It is an appealing illusion that we can control life, ourselves, and others through fixed structures, detailed planning, and the promise of rewards or threat of reprimands. But it is just that: an illusion. Research by Margaret Wheatley suggests that when we try to exert control in this way, it does more harm than good and drains a system of its vitality. It simply doesn't work. This is because human systems are complex, with many unseen and unknown dynamics and connections. Any change can create unintended consequences that can be nearly impossible to predict.

The same is true of environments that are uncertain and prone to disruption. In these environments, prescriptive rules are inappropriate at best and harmful at worst. And this is counter to traditional thinking about managing change. In his 1988 model of change, Harvard Professor John Kotter proposes that successful change lies in creating a burning platform, forming powerful coalitions, creating a vision, and then communicating that vision frequently and consistently. He suggests that a planned approach that progresses through identifiable stages of change is possible; that change happens at a constant and steady pace; and that at some point it stops so that we can draw breath and start our next 'campaign', ignite our next burning platform. But if any of that was ever true, it certainly isn't anymore.

In a volatile, complex environment, the impacts and consequences of decisions and actions are often unintended, unclear, or opaque; we just can't, don't, or won't see them. Rules are too narrow and prescriptive to work effectively in this kind of context. Instead, we need heuristics – practical guiding principles that help us solve problems and learn more about ourselves and others. Heuristic principles are not guaranteed to be optimal or perfect but are sufficient to reach an intermediate goal. They are rules of thumb that we know are imperfect, but that simplify things and make them easier to implement.

The six ROBUST principles outlined in Chapter 4 have been designed as guiding heuristics that can be applied across a range of contexts in your life, both personal and professional. They are flexible and expansive, not rigid or prescriptive. They meet the demands of a complex and changing environment and reveal a clear pathway forward.

3.

GETTING TO KNOW ANTIFRAGILE

IMAGINE YOU ARE ASKED TO CHAIR A MEETING AT THE LAST MINUTE because someone is sick. You've never chaired a meeting before and this is an important group of people in your world. Not surprisingly, you feel quite anxious about it.

There are a few ways you could respond to this situation:

1. You could say no and ask that someone else do it.

2. You could do it to the best of your ability, with varying degrees of success – some parts good, some less so – and spend the next few hours or days berating yourself about how awful you were and doing your best to put it out of your mind.

3. You could do it to the best of your ability, with varying degrees of success, ask for feedback from a few people at the meeting about what you did well and what you could improve on, and make a note of their comments along with your own reflections. You could then volunteer to do it again soon, incorporating what you've learned.

The opportunities for learning and growth that you gain from taking this third option mean there are more upsides than downsides to this random, unexpected opportunity to chair the meeting. And that's antifragile.

THE ANTIFRAGILE TEST

To understand whether something is fragile or antifragile, there is a simple test of symmetry we can apply: Anything that experiences more downsides than upsides from random events is fragile. Anything that experiences more upsides than downsides from random events is antifragile. So if you gain more from disruption, challenge, and change than you lose, you're antifragile.

ANTIFRAGILE ISN'T…

As we'll explore in one of the ROBUST principles later, it can be valuable to understand what something is *not*. We know now that antifragile is gaining more than you lose through randomness and disruption, but what is antifragile *not*?

Let's take a look.

Antifragile isn't doing it alone.

You may think that becoming antifragile is about being the 'hero', saving the day by taking everything on yourself. Not so much! As we'll explore later, there are many advantages to being part of a collective in terms of learning, wisdom, and distribution of risk.

Becoming antifragile is not a solo endeavour.

Antifragile isn't 'strong' – not in the traditional sense.

Many of us think of 'strong' as meaning solid, sturdy, and durable – like a lighthouse, able to withstand the elements. There is certainly strength

GETTING TO KNOW ANTIFRAGILE

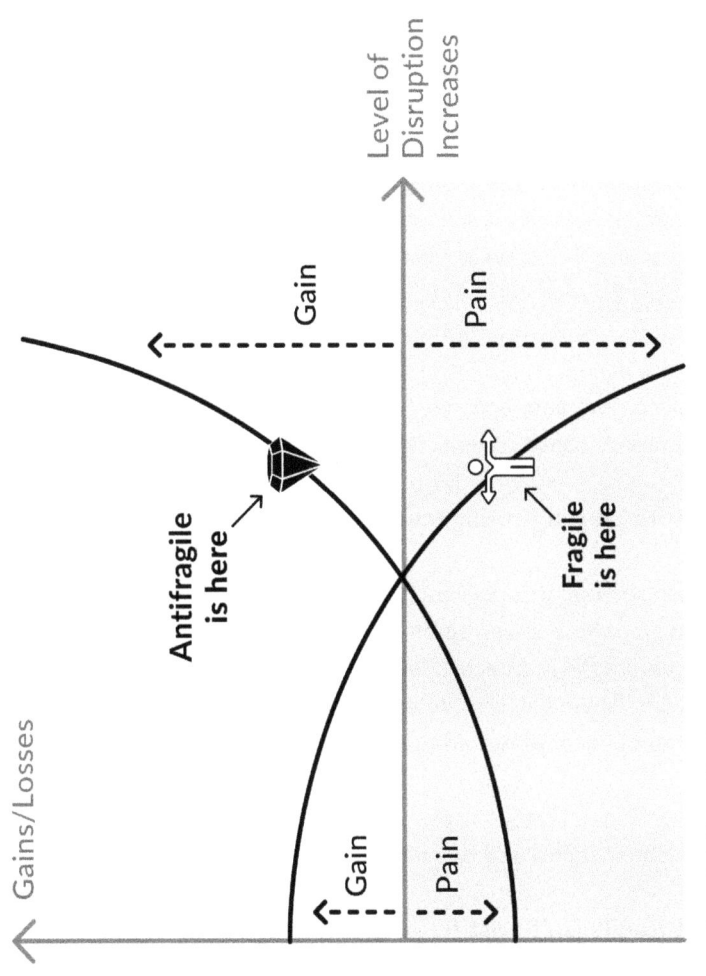

Figure 3.1: The antifragile test

in antifragility, and durability too, but of a different nature. Antifragility is not about being solid or sturdy; quite the opposite – it's about being flexible, agile, light on your feet.

Becoming antifragile is about embodying the strength of a ballet dancer rather than a weightlifter.

Antifragile isn't denying emotions.

It's easy to think that antifragile is about having a 'stiff upper lip', that showing emotions is a sign of weakness and we must keep all that 'messiness' inside. The thing is, what we feel in response to our experiences and the way we make sense of that is an important feedback loop that provides us with useful information and can be a valuable source of energy.

In becoming antifragile we harness 'the feels' and use them to move us towards constructive action.

Antifragile isn't resilience.

When something is resilient, it reacts to an event and is able to 'bounce back' to where it was before. And therein lies the difference. Becoming antifragile is an *active, intentional process* that allows us to *move beyond* where we were; to evolve, grow, and thrive through the experience of uncertainty, randomness, and disruption.

Becoming antifragile is about moving forward and making progress, not bouncing up and down only to come back to the same spot.

Antifragile isn't post-traumatic growth.

Post-traumatic growth (PTG) describes the idea that people who endure extreme adversity often see positive growth afterwards. It's acknowledged as a process that takes a lot of time, energy, and struggle because, at some level, the adversity has challenged the person's core beliefs. It involves considerable psychological work and may require professional support. While PTG is probably the closest idea we currently have in the social sciences to antifragility, it is not quite the same. Becoming antifragile looks to 'shrink' the experience of post-traumatic growth, both in terms of the scale of trauma and the time lag between experience and growth.

Becoming antifragile is 'micro-PTG' in real time.

THE BECOMING ANTIFRAGILE LANDSCAPE

Becoming antifragile is a journey of several stages. Let's get familiar with the landscape by defining our terms.

- **Disruption:** a disturbance that necessitates change and creates uncertainty, pressure, and challenge because of its impact on environmental conditions.
- **Thriving:** having the confidence, motivation, and support to deal with disruption.

We can think of the Becoming Antifragile journey on a continuum, from fragility through robustness to antifragility.

- **Fragile:** someone who *cannot cope* with the level of disruption in their environment.
- **Robust:** someone who can *withstand* the level of disruption in their environment.
- **Antifragile:** someone who *improves* through the level of disruption in their environment.

It is useful to understand that fragile and antifragile are relative terms rather than absolute. What that means is that just because you are more antifragile than your friend or colleague doesn't mean you *are* antifragile. Becoming antifragile is an ongoing journey of self-development. Even as you develop and build on your Antifragile Energy,

Attitudes, and Mindsets, there will always be room to become more antifragile – or more fragile.

The other thing to remember as we consider the Becoming Antifragile map is that your level of antifragility is the result of an *interaction* between the level of disruption you perceive in your world and your capacity to thrive through it, that is, your feelings of confidence and motivation and the support you have in dealing with the situations you face. This means you will likely have different levels of antifragility in different areas of your life. As an example, let's compare my 15-year-old daughter, Olivia, with my 82-year-old mother, Margaret. Liv is definitely more physically antifragile than my mum, but on a mental level, my mum – who grew up during World War II – is probably more antifragile than Liv, who has had a comfortable and pretty stable life – so far!

THE BECOMING ANTIFRAGILE MAP

You can see that the Becoming Antifragile map falls across two axes. The horizontal (x) axis represents the level of disruption, and the vertical (y) axis represents the level of thriving.

Let's explore the map together…

Low disruption, low thriving:
Surviving for now

On the bottom left of the map there is low disruption and low thriving. In these safe, simple, and stable situations where the environment is known, there is little need to be antifragile. Our fragility is not tested or exposed, and we are **surviving for now**. Here we may feel a level of ease, but at the back of our minds we know that this is temporary: we are working to our limits and our vulnerability could be exposed at any time.

GETTING TO KNOW ANTIFRAGILE

High thriving

Coping in comfort

Thriving through striving

Low disruption

High disruption

Surviving for now

Breaking under Pressure

Low thriving

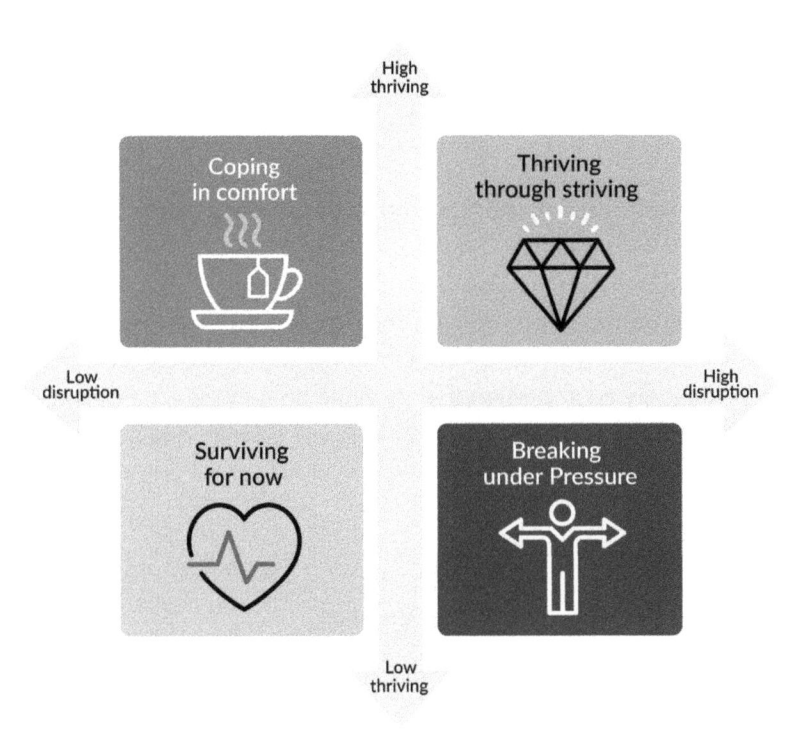

Figure 3.2: The Becoming Antifragile map

High disruption, low thriving:
Breaking under pressure

When disruption increases and our context becomes less familiar, less stable, more complex, and more uncertain, our fragility is tested and the need for us to be antifragile kicks in. In these settings, if we have low levels of thriving we are fragile and can **break under pressure**. As I'm sure we've all experienced, breaking is painful. We struggle to cope with what's being asked of us and can't see a path to the resources we need to get through.

Low disruption, high thriving:
Living in comfort

If volatility in our environment is manageable and we have a higher level of thriving we can be **living in comfort**. Being here feels good, and it can be an important and valuable time to reflect and consolidate learning. However, complex adaptive systems need challenge to grow and thrive so if we stay here too long, we risk becoming stagnant and falling back into 'surviving for now' – perhaps without even realising it.

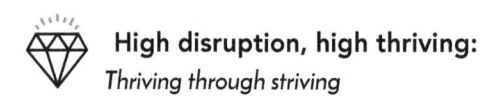

High disruption, high thriving:
Thriving through striving

When we have good levels of confidence, motivation, and support to deal with the higher levels of disruption in our environment we are becoming antifragile. Here, we are **thriving through striving** as we try new ways of being and doing, assess what works and what doesn't, and adjust our plans and actions accordingly. This doesn't always feel comfortable; in fact, it often doesn't. Striving requires courage, tenacity, and the right energy, attitudes, and mindsets – and maintaining these can be exhausting. Being in this space can feel like a roller coaster as you ride the ups and downs of growth and development in response to – or to keep ahead of – volatility in your context. This does come with a risk of burnout. To counter this, we may intentionally move to 'living in comfort', at least in some areas of our life, in order to create the time, space, and energy to keep going.

LOCATING YOUR POSITION ON THE MAP

We now know that whether you are fragile, robust, or antifragile depends on two things: the level of disruption you perceive in your world, and your capacity to thrive through it. You can find out where you are on the map at www.theantifragilesurvey.com. Here you can also get a personalised report on your Antifragile Energy, Attitudes, and Mindsets and your use of the ROBUST principles. Even though we haven't covered these concepts yet, it's a good idea to do this now so you get an idea of the starting point for your Becoming Antifragile journey.

As we learn to navigate and use the experiences of disruption and discomfort to grow, develop, and even transform, we learn to thrive. By first reducing and removing fragility and then learning to embrace struggle by using challenging experiences as learning opportunities, we become antifragile. As a result, we experience less stress and anxiety, feel better, are more productive, and have higher 'performance' across all areas of life. And we lead better, too – ourselves, our teams, and the people we care for.

Be warned though, this doesn't happen overnight! It is a dynamic, iterative, 'three steps forward, two steps back' kind of journey. It is not something you tick off; it is never 'done'. We continually become antifragile as disruption and change present us with new challenges and opportunities in our volatile and uncertain context. And as we do, we learn new skills and gain new knowledge about ourselves, others, and the world around us. These are the nutrients that help us grow, nourish our development, and provide the tools for our ongoing journey.

SUMMARY

» The simple antifragile test is: If something gains more from randomness, disruption, and change than it loses, it is antifragile. If it loses more than it gains, it is fragile.

» It is useful to understand what antifragile isn't. Antifragile isn't a solo endeavour; it isn't being strong or denying emotions; it goes beyond resilience; and it is different to post-traumatic growth.

» The Becoming Antifragile map plots levels of disruption (uncertainty, challenge, and change) against levels of thriving (confidence, motivation, and support).

» Where you stand on the fragility-robustness-antifragility continuum depends on the interaction between the level of disruption you perceive in your world and your capacity to thrive through it.

» There are four general areas to the Becoming Antifragile map:

   1. Low disruption, low thriving: Surviving for now

   2. High disruption, low thriving: Breaking under pressure

   3. Low disruption, high thriving: Living in comfort

   4. High disruption, high thriving: Thriving through striving

» You can locate your position on the map at www.theantifragilesurvey.com.

» Becoming antifragile doesn't happen overnight and can feel uncomfortable. It requires courage, tenacity, and the right energy, attitudes, and mindsets.

REFERENCES

Part II Introduction
Research by Margaret Wheatley suggests... Wheatley, M. J. (1992). *Leadership and the New Science: Discovering Order in a Chaotic World.* San Francisco, CA: Berrett-Koehler.

Chapter 3
To understand whether something is fragile or antifragile, there is a simple test of symmetry we can apply... Taleb, N. N. (2013). *Antifragile: Things That Gain from Disorder.* London, UK: Penguin.

LIVING THE DREAM

Alex's partner Charlie sat down in the study and looked out the window to the garden. The grass really needed cutting and those weeds in the veggie patch were seriously out of control! This weekend had been a write-off in terms of getting to the garden – a mad rush of housework, shopping, birthday parties, and play dates. And the fact that Alex had worked for three hours on Saturday hadn't helped.

Charlie was feeling the pressure of work too. Taking the chance to leap out of the corporate world with the unexpected offer of redundancy 10 months ago had seemed like such a good idea. After all, creating a start-up would mean no boss, the ability to follow your own energy and creativity, and the opportunity to do work you love with people you like, with flexibility to work when and where you wanted…. wouldn't it? Well, that was the dream – but the reality didn't quite measure up. The pressure of doing everything, literally *everything* the business needed – from sales and marketing to accounts and admin – felt overwhelming. And of course, the bills still had to be paid. They had talked about that just last night – as the kids got older they were getting 'more expensive to run', as Alex had put it, and whilst the business was going well for a solopreneur start-up, it certainly wasn't bringing in the corporate salary they'd been used to.

Charlie was thinking about diversifying – trying some new products and services with current clients, taking existing lines into new markets. The meetings with people in the industry last week had been exhausting but had really paid off; they'd suggested testing things out for the next few months and see what landed before making a big commitment. Charlie felt excited by the prospect, but also nervous – what if none of it worked? Well, there was still the option of teaching evening classes at the local community centre, Charlie thought. Not the most exciting work, but it would bring in enough to keep food on the table – even if it was only baked beans on toast!

WHAT DO YOU SEE?

- Charlie is taking several steps towards becoming antifragile. What are they?

- In what areas of your life do you feel you are robust? Antifragile? What is your evidence?

- What are you doing to support your robustness or antifragility?

4.

GUIDING PRINCIPLES TO BECOMING ANTIFRAGILE

THERE ARE SIX PRINCIPLES TO GUIDE YOU ON YOUR JOURNEY TO becoming antifragile. The first letter of each principle spells the word ROBUST, hence the 'ROBUST principles'. Generally speaking I'm not a fan of acronyms, but our brains love them because they help us remember complex information easily, which saves processing time. And as you'll find out, working with the brain rather than against it is foundational to becoming antifragile.

THE ROBUST PRINCIPLES

When we build a house, we start with the foundations. And so it is with the ROBUST framework. The first principle, *Recruit the Brain*, is based on what we know about how the brain works and how this influences everything we think, feel, and do. Understanding the physiological processes and responses in your brain is critical for leading yourself and others effectively. The next step is to understand the tricks your mind can play on you so you can recognise and stop self-sabotage in its tracks. This is what the *Operate in Reality* principle is all about. The next two principles, *Break the Negative* and *Use Intelligent Risk*, explore what's holding you back, what can help you succeed, and how to be a smart innovator in your own life and leadering. The final two principles, *Seek Collective Wisdom* and *Tackle the Infinite Game*, examine

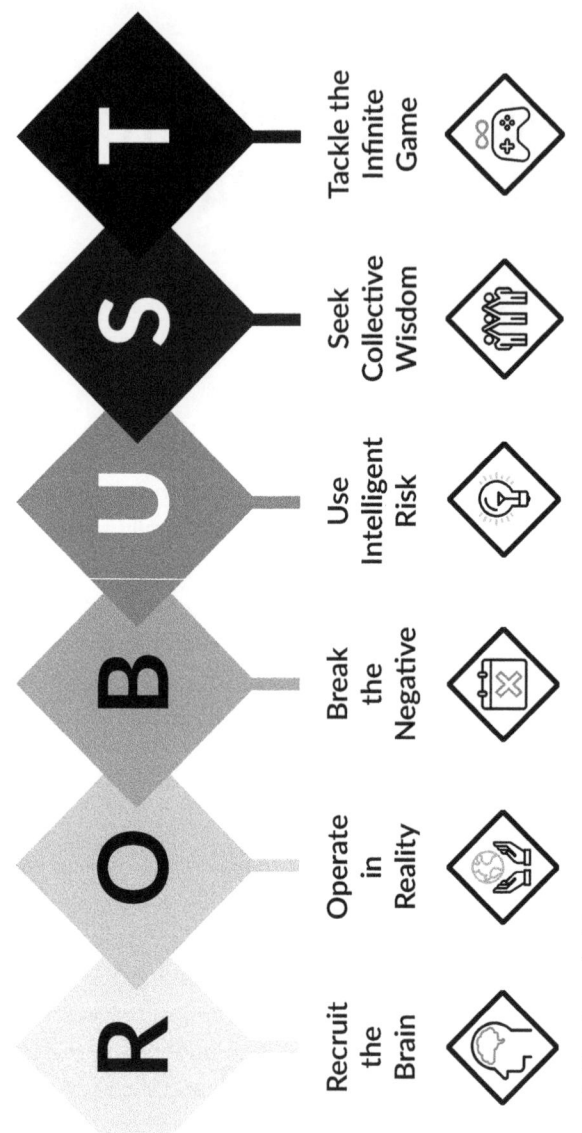

Figure 4.1: The robust principles

- R — Recruit the Brain
- O — Operate in Reality
- B — Break the Negative
- U — Use Intelligent Risk
- S — Seek Collective Wisdom
- T — Tackle the Infinite Game

why becoming antifragile is not a solo endeavour. We need others to learn, to connect, and to give us a purpose beyond ego for our efforts.

PUTTING THE ROBUST PRINCIPLES INTO PRACTICE

In my work with leaders and teams, as well as in my own leadering, I've found that questions are the quickest, most effective way to get to the heart of the work that needs to be done. Questions are agile, flexible, and easy to use. They focus our attention and our conversations, which in turn determines our planning and our actions. They encourage us to pause and ponder, to stay curious and reflective, and to keep exploring and learning. Each ROBUST principle provides you with one or more 'hacks' in the form of a question or questions to ask yourself or others. Play with the language to make it work for you, but keep asking! These questions will help you bring the ROBUST principles to life in whatever context you are facing. They will help you become antifragile.

PRINCIPLE 1: RECRUIT THE BRAIN

'I want to live happily in a world I don't understand.'
– NASSIM NICHOLAS TALEB

The study of the brain, neuroscience, covers brain function at every level, from the basic unit – single neurons – through to complex neural networks that govern our every thought and action. Neuroscience has progressed in leaps and bounds in the last decade as technologies such as functional MRI have enabled us to actually visualise the way the brain works, offering us new ways to understand our experiences and manage them more effectively. Researchers can now 'watch' the brain in action, and this is providing powerful insights into cognitive and behavioural processes and the interrelation between mind and body.

By understanding how the brain and mind work, we can be strategic, hack the short circuits, and get out of our own way. I can't think of a more powerful foundation from which to become antifragile.

Safety first

The brain is at the centre of everything we do. It is our central processing unit and our memory bank. It determines what's stored on our hard drive and what's shown on our video card, and it acts as our motherboard, sending signals to other parts of our system. It also drives our emotions – and neuroscientists are beginning to understand more about the biological changes that take place in our brains as certain emotions are triggered.

A critical concept to understand about the brain on your journey to becoming antifragile is that its organising principle is to 'minimise danger, maximise reward'. This is the filter through which the brain processes every piece of incoming data and assesses how we should respond, moment to moment.

'Negativity bias' is a psychological phenomenon whereby we pay more attention to and give more weight to negative experiences or information than positive ones. For example, you can probably recall unpleasant childhood experiences more easily than pleasant ones (I clearly remember when our dog ate my birthday cake for my fifth birthday, but I'm hazy on the many other wonderful birthday parties I had as a child!), and it is often the negative experiences of the day rather than the positive that replay in your mind as you're trying to get to sleep.

Negativity bias is, in essence, a mechanism to try to keep us safe. From an evolutionary perspective, it makes sense that we pay attention to threats and problems that could have implications for our safety or survival. But what makes sense in evolutionary terms may not be as adaptive in your current circumstances. After all, it is unlikely you will meet a sabre-toothed tiger on your way to work, or a poisonous snake in your office!

Whilst challenges with colleagues, pressing deadlines, and productivity problems may feel like life and death in the moment, they really aren't – so a hardwired survival mechanism that diverts our attention towards threats and problems may not translate well into our 21st-century lives. In fact, it has been shown that negativity bias reduces life satisfaction and increases anxiety and depression. This is why allowing our negativity bias to have free rein can make us fragile.

> RECRUIT THE BRAIN HACK:
> **Challenge your negativity bias.**
> *Ask: What's working well here?*

Manage the feels

Negativity bias and the brain's concern with keeping us safe can lead us to react strongly to situations that our brain considers to be risky. When this happens, it activates one of the oldest parts of our brain: the 'amygdala'. The amygdala sends a cocktail of neurotransmitters into the brain, which triggers physiological and psychological reactions – the classic fight, flight, or freeze responses. This ancient part of the brain is driven purely by emotion. It has no capacity for language or processing, but is great at recognising threat and responding to keep you alive. Unfortunately, there is no dimmer switch on the fight-or-flight circuit – it's either on or off!

The newest part of our brain – the prefrontal cortex – is what distinguishes us from most other mammals. It gives us the capacity for language and cognitive processing, so that we can assess situations, decide the level of threat, and respond accordingly. The older part of our brain *reacts*, the newer part *responds*. Both are critical for our survival, and understanding how they talk to each other can help us be more effective in challenging situations. By integrating the old and the new, we can reduce the amount of negative stress we experience.

When the amygdala is 'triggered', the potent cocktail of cortisol and adrenaline flooding through our neural pathways means that 'peripheral' systems, such as hearing and cognitive processing, are compromised. At its most extreme, this response doesn't just impair peripheral systems – it hijacks them, taking them offline completely. If you've ever seen a tantruming toddler, you've seen this type of brain hijack in full force! By this stage, there is very little activity going on in the prefrontal cortex and you are effectively just one big ball of emotional reaction. As I'm sure you can imagine, this is not a good place to be for you, your goals, or the people you're with.

All is not lost, however! If we can tune in and catch the early warning signs that come before the 'hijack' takes hold, we can avert it. As we've mentioned, in the modern world, it's unlikely you are going to have to face a sabre-toothed tiger. Cognitively, you know that in most situations there is no true threat to your life. The problem is, your new brain doesn't assess the *real* external situation – it assesses what you are thinking and feeling. So when you *perceive* a threat in your environment, whether it's real or not, your 'new brain' sends signals to your 'old brain' to trigger the fight-or-flight response. Can you see the issue? The threat response often occurs not in response to a *true* external threat, but merely to the *perception* of it – and that means it can happen at any time.

Once the new brain has thrown the match on the fight-or-flight response, it uses its considerable logic and processing capacity to justify and rationalise the physical response we experience – raised heart rate, sweating, shallow breathing, blood rushing to our limbs to prepare us to run away or stand and fight – and this leads to a feedback loop of stress.

The good news is that this loop is controllable. If you can become aware of the early warning signs of your stress response, including the physical changes, you can choose to engage your new brain to help your stress response rather than hinder it. A simple way to do this is to take three deep breaths that fill your belly as well as your chest. This floods your brain with oxygen, which triggers a release of calming endorphins. The trick is to catch your early warning signals *before* your fight-or-flight response has been triggered.

> RECRUIT THE BRAIN HACK:
> **Be a stress detective.**
>
> *When you feel yourself getting stressed,
> ask: What am I feeling and where?*

Focus, focus, focus

The 'wiring' of our brains also explains why motivation can be such a fickle friend, and understanding how this works can reveal some great hacks to help us become antifragile and achieve goal success.

When we set goals, we immediately channel our attention. In its default state, the brain is noisy, with dozens of fleeting thoughts swarming around our own internal narrative. When we focus our attention, we redirect these random neural firing patterns to form focused pathways committed to addressing the current challenge, whether that's completing a report by midday or deciding what to cook for dinner. Of all the possible ways in which we could deploy our energy, we focus on directing it towards the achievement of a specific and measurable goal. And this helps us achieve success.

Why?

An interesting change occurs when we consciously focus on a goal: the brain develops a kind of 'filter'. It subconsciously evaluates information in our environment to determine which information is goal-relevant. Like a radar, it notices incoming data that may contribute to or influence goal achievement, and selectively focuses our attention on that data. At the same time, it filters out irrelevant information to protect our brain from cognitive overload.

So what's the lesson from this?

Intentionally set and focus on your goals. When you do, your brain will filter and focus incoming information in such a way as to help you achieve them – almost without trying!

But once you've consciously focused on your goals, how can you hack your brain to stay motivated towards achieving them?

To ensure our survival, subconscious systems have evolved to balance our choices in certain ways. At a fundamental level, our most powerful motivator is fear. However, research suggests that it is not the most *effective* motivator in terms of achieving long-term outcomes. When we are motivated by fear of a perceived danger or threat, we want to move *away* from it. This is what psychologists call 'avoidance motivation'. Avoidance responses in our brain trigger the fight-or-flight response, which, as we've already covered, reduces our ability to think and process information, as well as our capacity for self-awareness and emotional regulation. As we become more defensive, the brain's heightened need for safety can lead us to misjudge situations and people as threats.

Of course, the brain is also motivated by reward – opportunities for growth, learning, and connection. When we are motivated in this way, we want to move *towards* something. Evidence suggests that when we have this 'approach motivation', we stick with goals for longer, and so achieve greater success.

So what can we learn from this?

When you're setting goals, think about the language you are using. Rather than framing a goal through an avoidance lens – what you want to avoid – reframe it to the more positive approach lens. What is it you want to achieve or move towards?

> RECRUIT THE BRAIN HACK:
> **Know what you want.**
>
> *Ask: What do I want more of in my life?*
> *What do I want to work towards?*

PRINCIPLE 2: OPERATE IN REALITY

'My idea of the modern stoic sage is someone who transforms fear into prudence, pain into information, mistakes into initiation, and desire into undertaking.'
– NASSIM NICHOLAS TALEB

Be stoic

As leaders, we're often told to 'bring more of ourselves' to work and to get comfortable showing our emotions so that our people feel they can do the same. And, as a general principle, this can certainly be helpful – particularly if we view emotions as information that helps us assess and adjust our actions to make the best possible contribution to the situation in front of us. But as we've just covered, and as I've seen over and over in my work with senior leadership teams, there are also times when emotion clouds our perspective and can derail us from making progress. This is when stoic leadership can serve us well.

Stoicism is a branch of ancient Western philosophy that explores attitudes to life, self-leadership, and risk. The thing I really enjoy about Stoicism is that it is practical and straightforward. At its core are three simple lessons:

- The world is unpredictable, and life is brief.
- Satisfaction and achievement come from being steadfast, strong, and in control.
- Dissatisfaction comes from impulsive reflexes rather than logic.

Stoicism looks to transform unhelpful negative emotions by applying perspective and realism, and taking effective action based on that assessment. Stoic exercises such as 'practising' misfortune and poverty help teach us that the worst-case scenario we are thinking of is not, in fact, the worst possible, and often not the most likely. It also helps us to avoid getting too attached to our external circumstances or the various forms of 'wealth' – status, money, material possessions, and so on – and to understand that they may be taken away at any time by the randomness of life.

An important aspect of *Operating in Reality* is understanding what is in your control and what isn't so that you can respond effectively. Epictetus, a prominent Stoic philosopher in the first and second centuries, is understood to have said, 'The chief task in life is simply this: to identify and separate matters so that I can say clearly to myself which are externals, not under my control, and which have to do with the choice I actually control.'

I teach leaders a four-step process that takes less than two minutes to help them put Epictetus' wise words into practice by assessing the situation and taking effective action based in reality:

Step 1: Take three deep belly breaths to flood your brain with oxygen and keep it out of fight-or-flight mode.

Step 2: Get a piece of paper and draw four columns: *Can't*, *Can*, *Influence*, and *Action*. This helps keep your brain in logical-rational mode rather than emotional-spiralling mode.

Step 3: In the first column, identify what about the situation you *can't control*; in the second, what you *can control*; and in the third, what you *can influence*. Filling in the 'can't control' column first will help you get out the stuff that's really bothering you so that you can think more effectively in columns 2 and 3. It will also help you be clear about what is 'on the table' for discussion (i.e. what can be controlled/influenced) in your meetings and conversations.

Step 4: Review columns 2 and 3 – what you can control and what you can influence – and, on that basis, complete column 4 with *action you can take*.

Can't	Can	Influence	Actions

Figure 4.2: Getting clear on your control, influence, and actions

I recommend that you write this down, but you can do it internally as a thought process if the situation requires it. You can also use it as a coaching conversation with a team member, whereby you ask the questions, talk through the process, and find answers together.

> OPERATE IN REALITY HACK:
> **Be a control freak.**
>
> *Ask: What can't I control? What can I control? What can I influence?*

Limit the leakage

Workplace drama researcher Cy Wakeman suggests that the average company wastes up to 900 hours a year on emotional 'drama', much of which is driven by our internal stories. Humans are sense-making creatures, and one way in which we try to make sense of the world is to create stories that we tell ourselves about what's happening. Whilst some of these stories are accurate, many are not. Because of this, it's important to be able to recognise faulty thinking in your stories so that you can challenge them when they are unhelpful.

The trouble is, our brains simply don't have the capacity to process all the information that is available to us. In fact, of the 11 million pieces of information that our senses receive every second, we can only consciously process around 40. That means we are only ever getting a very limited, filtered view of our environment. The 'reality' we experience depends on where we place our attention, and therefore what bits of information our brain processes. So at any given moment, our 'reality' is just one of infinite possibilities.

Looking for alternatives is one way to expand the information being processed by the brain, move away from a fear-based perspective, and challenge irrational assumptions about the way things should or shouldn't be. When you find yourself locked into an unhelpful story, the sentence starters below can help you challenge that story and expand your perspective:

- Another, more accurate way to see this is…
- That's not entirely true, because there's also evidence that…
- I need to put this in perspective; the most likely outcome is… and I can do… to help me deal with it.

Another useful way to challenge your unhelpful stories is to ask, *What would I tell a friend in this situation?*

It's important to remember that not *every* thought that leads to an uncomfortable feeling is unhelpful or inaccurate. Negative emotions like fear, guilt, sadness, and anger can provide valuable information about what is going on in our lives. Feelings and emotions are *information*, and if we use them as such, even the uncomfortable ones can provide us with valuable signals and motivate us to change our behaviour.

As you open your mind to alternative stories to explain your challenge/situation, notice the changes in how you are feeling and what you feel able to do. Which story serves you best to achieve the outcomes that you want? Which story boosts your resilience and enables you to engage with the situation and move forward constructively?

The four questions in this next hack come from Byron Katie's *The Work* and always help me cut through my storytelling.

> OPERATE IN REALITY HACK:
> **Find the fairy tale.**
>
> *Ask: Is it true? Can I absolutely know that it is true? Who am I when I believe that story? Who would I be without it?*

Be present

For us to *Operate in Reality*, we need to be *in* reality, and that means being in the present moment. Unfortunately, the modern workplace is addicted to activity, speed, and short-term outcomes – and the result is a culture that celebrates multitasking and generates mindlessness.

It *is* possible to multitask. In effect, we're doing it all the time: cooking a meal whilst watching television, or taking down notes whilst listening to a presentation. This impressive capability can be attributed to the basal ganglia in your brain – a complex set of subcortical structures that store your life experiences and create and maintain your habits.

Unfortunately, it is the prefrontal cortex, not the basal ganglia, that holds current information in working memory, consciously processes that information, and deals with new or complex issues. There is no autopilot here. And whilst the basal ganglia can draw on almost unlimited capacity, the prefrontal cortex has limited daily capacity and struggles constantly with what to prioritise and bring to conscious thought. Studies have shown that performance deteriorates significantly as soon as we attempt more than one cognitively taxing task at a time. Try reading an article while watching the news, or adding a list of numbers while someone is speaking to you.

With that in mind, let's bust some myths about multitasking.

Myth: *Multitasking makes you more productive.*

Fact: Each additional task you undertake concurrently with others reduces your performance on all tasks.

Multitasking diffuses attention, compromises memory, and reduces performance. Despite workplace pressure to the contrary, multitasking can be, and in many cases is, an impediment to performance.

Myth: *You can rebound quickly from distractions.*

Fact: It can take up to 15 minutes to restore concentration following a distraction, due to a refractory period in the brain.

A temporary shift in attention from one task to another – when an email alert pings, or when someone stops at your desk – increases the amount of time necessary to finish the primary task by as much as 25%. This phenomenon, known as 'switching time', drains our mental energy and makes it harder to get back to the task at hand.

The brain is simply not designed for multitasking. So in a world brimming with distractions, what's the antidote?

Mindfulness.

Mindfulness is the nurturing of focus in the present moment, connecting with the sensory environment and giving awareness to the now. When we are mindful, we are tuned in to the people, conversations, and accompanying emotions right here, right now. We are 'in the moment', and therefore in reality. There are many benefits to mindfulness, including reduced physiological and psychological stress, improved emotional regulation, and increased overall wellbeing. Recent research with engineers also suggests that mindfulness practice improves both creativity and problem-solving skills.

Unfortunately, the truth is we spend much of each day *mindlessly* half-listening to conversations, multitasking numerous activities, and reactively following the bouncing ball as one distraction after another derails us. Mindfulness is the perfect antidote to this mindlessness, as it requires focused attention and concentration.

Dr. Shauna Shapiro suggests a practical model of mindfulness practice that can be applied at any time of day. It involves three steps:

1. Identify your **intention**. Why you are doing what you're doing, and what outcome are you seeking?
2. Focus your **attention**. What are you paying attention to, and what distractions are you putting aside?
3. Understand your **attitude**. How, in this moment, are you paying attention – with acceptance, openness, curiosity?

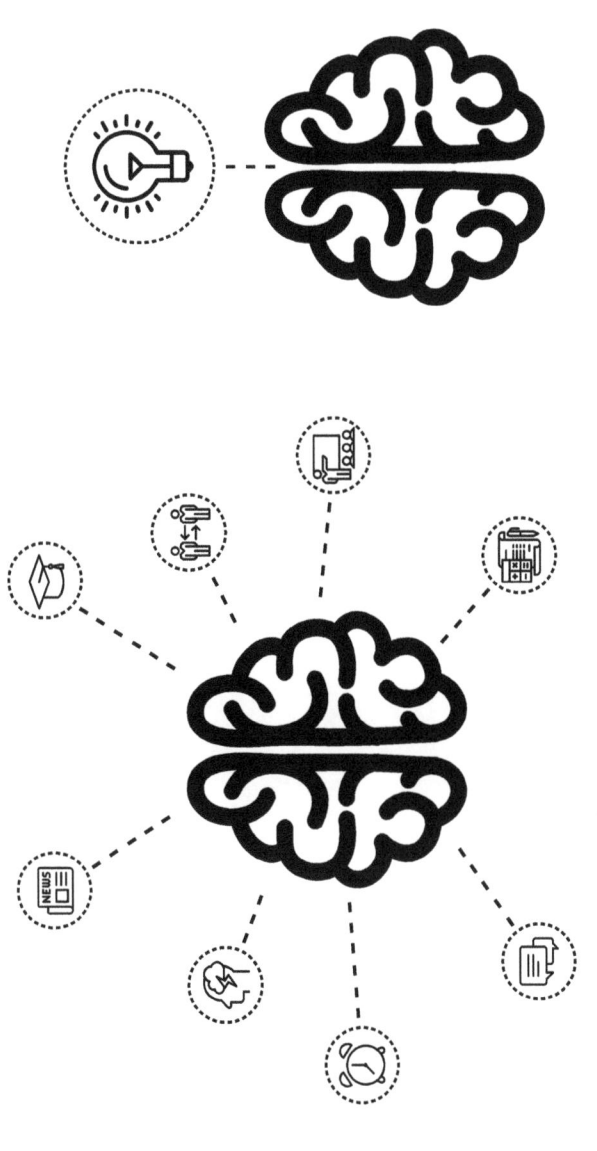

Figure 4.3: Mindfulness is the antidote to distraction.

The thing I really like about this model of mindfulness practice is that you can use it to focus your attention at any point during the day – when you get to your desk in the morning, when you walk into a meeting, as you walk into the house at the end of the day, or whenever you need to ground yourself. By doing so, you will truly *Operate in Reality*.

> OPERATE IN REALITY HACK:
> **Be mindful.**
>
> *Ask: Why am I here? Where is my focus? How am I showing up?*

PRINCIPLE 3: BREAK THE NEGATIVE, BUILD THE POSITIVE

> *'Increasing happiness is fragile, decreasing known sources of unhappiness is antifragile.'*
> – NASSIM NICHOLAS TALEB

Take the 'via negativa'

Now that we have an understanding of the internal Operating System – iOS – of our brain and mind, we have the foundations from which to become antifragile. But, as we covered in Part I, to become antifragile we need to remove fragility. In fact, removing fragility is the very *first thing* we need to do to clear the way for building robustness and becoming antifragile. So this is the time for us to ask ourselves: *What's* not *working?*

Despite the convenience of modern life drawing us towards a slothful existence, humans are inherently action oriented. Motivation is a primal instinct as we scan our environments and look to make them safe and secure. We are predisposed to solve problems, prevent threats, and take action.

Because of this, we want to *do* more – we want to intervene because that gives us a sense of control. But this is not always helpful.

When asked about his approach to sculpting his masterpiece *David*, Michelangelo is famously quoted as saying, 'I took an unfinished block of marble and simply removed everything that wasn't *David*.' Whether or not this story is true, it is a useful metaphor for what is known as 'via negativa' — the idea of arriving at the desired outcome by way of what it is *not*.

'Non-doing' is an action that has as much inherent value and as many side effects as 'doing'. Unfortunately, choosing to 'not do' often goes unnoticed and is generally undervalued. However, there is clear merit in *not* doing something negative, as this will always lead to a more positive outcome. An obvious example of this is smoking. All other things being equal, the most direct way for a smoker to improve their health is to stop smoking. They could choose to take other positive health behaviours – improve their diet, exercise regularly, etc. – but if they kept smoking, there would be a ceiling to the impact of those efforts.

Another advantage of 'non-doing' is that it doesn't have the domino effect of unintended consequences that can come with 'taking action'. Let's go back to our friend the smoker: they could choose to deal with their smoking by chewing gum or wearing patches, but the side effects of these could also have negative health implications. This action, though clearly well intentioned, could potentially create more and different health issues.

I like to think of via negativa as 'smart avoidance'. Rather than taking action to solve a problem, ask yourself how or if you could remove or avoid an underlying cause of the problem. Of course, to understand what we need to remove or avoid, we need to imagine how choosing to 'not do' an action will affect the situation: how we can take the via negativa to remove or avoid what is making us fragile. Unfortunately, it's not always easy to recognise what's making us fragile. Our habits of thinking, feeling, and doing are often so deeply embedded in our leading that they are barely conscious. In order to uncover our fragilities and take action to remove their causes, we need to dig deep.

There are two approaches we can take to this: removing unhelpful habits, and avoiding creating bad habits.

Remove unhelpful habits

Remember that the brain's primary function is to keep us safe and that it filters all the information we receive through that lens, with a negativity bias. The challenge is that this makes it easy to unconsciously fall into habits that lead us to 'play small to stay safe' – and this makes us fragile.

In my work with leaders (and in reflecting on my own leading) I've come to recognise three failures that drive unhelpful habits and obstruct the path to becoming antifragile:

1. **Failure to listen.** Do you get to answers before other people and (maybe secretly) think that you have the best ideas in the room?
2. **Failure to learn.** Do you repeat the same mistakes rather than reflecting and learning from what doesn't go well?
3. **Failure to lean in.** Do you have the confidence to speak up, go against the flow of conversation, and lean in to your leadership?

In thinking about your responses to these questions, identify at least three examples in the past week that you can use as evidence to support your answer. Remember, habits are embedded patterns of behaviour, so if you can't think of three examples in the last seven days, then it's probably not a habit. And don't let yourself off the hook! It can be easy to pretend that you do all the right stuff, but you can't know what to remove until you get a clear look at it. Many of us have a 'to do' list – well, this is about creating your 'not to do' list.

> BREAK THE NEGATIVE HACK:
> ### Create a 'not to do' list.
> *Ask: What am I not going to do?*

Avoid creating bad habits

Our brains love the negative, and often the best way to get clear about an issue is to address it backwards. The great German algebraist Carl Jacobi said that the best way to approach difficult math problems is to 'Invert. Always invert.' And the same may be true here.

Rather than removing the negative, simply avoid it in the first place.

Steve Jobs understood the power of avoidance. When asked about innovation in an interview a few years ago, he replied, 'People think focus means saying yes to the thing you've to focus on. But that's not what it means at all. It means saying no to the hundred other good ideas that there are. You have to pick carefully. I'm actually as proud of the things we haven't done as the things I have done. Innovation is saying no to 1,000 things.'

So what will you say no to?

Think about the people that you consider to be fragile (it's often easier to see it in others than ourselves!). What do they do that makes them and keeps them fragile? Make a list of these things, because they're the things you're saying 'no' to.

BREAK THE NEGATIVE HACK:
Have an anti–role model.

Ask: What kind of leader do I not want to be?

If there are things in your life that are making you fragile, remove them, and avoid bringing more in. Reducing and avoiding fragile habits will have immediate and noticeable gains that you just won't get purely by taking positive actions.

Think positive

'Hang on, hang on!' I hear you cry. 'You've just told us to focus removing on the negative, but that sounds a lot like avoidance motivation, which you told us doesn't work. What gives?'

You're right. Via negativa hooks into avoidance motivation, which as we covered earlier can be fear based and often less effective than approach motivation in helping us achieve our long-term goals. So alongside our via negativa, we also need to build a 'via positiva' by focusing on the positives and using our strengths.

Positive thinking sounds fluffy and often gets a bad rap. But when we take a closer look at positive thinking, or optimism, you'll see that its impact is far from fluffy.

Let's be clear: optimism isn't about ignoring the bad stuff. Optimism is a hopeful, confident style and habit of thinking that influences how we explain, interpret, and think about ourselves and the world around us. And it can be developed through skill building – just like learning to play the guitar.

Particularly relevant to becoming antifragile is *realistic, flexible* optimism, which helps us to understand when to use optimistic versus pessimistic thinking styles, and how to adapt those styles in order to approach situations realistically. Realistic optimism involves hoping, aspiring, and searching for positive experiences whilst acknowledging what we do not know and accepting what we cannot know.

In dealing with ambiguous and uncertain situations, the realistic, flexible optimist hopes for and works towards desired outcomes, and does not expect them to occur without dedicated effort to bring them about. They focus on how to create opportunities to *increase* the likelihood of achieving outcomes, whilst working within realistic boundaries and the constraints of the current situation.

Realistic, flexible optimism is not about self-deception. Quite the opposite: it requires us to take regular reality checks to monitor progress, assess potential opportunities, and re-evaluate planned next steps. It requires us to pay attention to feedback from other people and our environment to gauge whether our hopes and beliefs are in the range of plausible positive possibilities. And if they're not, we flex and adjust accordingly.

> BUILD THE POSITIVE HACK:
> **Nurture your inner optimist.**
>
> *Ask: What's the best I can hope for given what I know right now?*

Harness strengths

Research suggests that, in most workplaces, we spend around 80% of our time talking about problems and just 20% discussing what's working well. Now, as leaders, we drive the agenda for lots of conversations in the workplace, and this should prompt us to take a good look at ourselves.

Do you focus on problems rather than harnessing strengths?

Come on, be honest now…

Yes, I know we've got the negativity bias to contend with, but the thing is, talking and thinking about what's working creates opportunities for us to enjoy what is right, and to focus on abilities instead of inabilities. It encourages people to think in terms of strengths rather than weaknesses, and to concentrate on capacities rather than shortcomings. All the evidence suggests that we get to our highest performance by building strengths rather than fixing weaknesses. Why is that?

Strengths reflect the way your brain is naturally wired to perform at its best. The neural pathways that support your strengths are well established, which makes using them easy, effective, and enjoyable. It's like driving on a six-lane freeway rather than an unsurfaced country road – there's simply more 'neural infrastructure' to support your performance.

It also feels good to use our strengths. They leave us feeling more confident, energised, and satisfied with ourselves and the outcomes we achieve. Studies show that people who use their strengths regularly are less stressed, more confident, happier, more energetic, and more satisfied, engaged, and creative at work. And it's for all these reasons that using strengths is an important part of the via positiva towards becoming antifragile. After all, when we're facing down disruption, challenge, and change, who wouldn't like a bit more confidence, energy, and creativity?

Researchers recommend we spend at least 80% of our time focusing on strengths.

To capitalise on how your brain is wired to perform at its best, researchers recommend that we flip the 80:20 ratio to spend at least 80% of our time building on our strengths. But how do you know what your strengths are?

Our strengths generally show up in the things we're good at and enjoy doing – the things we look forward to doing at work, home, or play. These can include both character strengths and talent strengths.

Character strengths are often aligned to your values and represent *how* you like to work. They are the 'essence of you' – those positive personality traits that you'll use even if you don't receive reward or recognition for them; things like hope, humour, gratitude, and perseverance. You can discover your character strengths using the free 10-minute survey at www.viacharacter.org.

Talent strengths take you towards high performance at work and are more about *what* you like to do. Talents are innate abilities that can be developed into strengths through intentional, sustained effort. You can discover your talents through a paid 20-minute survey at gallup-strengthscentre.com.

'But what about weaknesses?' I hear you ask. 'We can't just ignore them.'

You're absolutely right. And building the positive doesn't mean you ignore your weaknesses. But remember, fixing a weakness involves building 'brain infrastructure' in the form of new neural pathways – and that takes time, effort, and commitment. So be realistic. Perhaps a smarter approach is to first see if there is a strength you can develop to help you become antifragile and focus on reinforcing those existing pathways. If there's not, *then* be willing to address the weakness head on. Just be sure you have the support you need to deliver the outcomes you're after.

> BUILD THE POSITIVE HACK:
> **Leverage your strengths.**
> *Ask: How can I use my strengths to meet this challenge?*

PRINCIPLE 4: USE INTELLIGENT RISK

'Trial and error is freedom.'
– NASSIM NICHOLAS TALEB

One of the things that can make us fragile as leaders is a reluctance to try new ways of being, doing, and leading. It's no surprise. Our brains are wired to keep us safe, and trying something new can feel risky. But research has found the leaders who champion innovation, challenge standard approaches, and lead change are rated significantly more positively by their teams, peers, and bosses in terms of their leadership effectiveness. Not only that, but innovation is essential to tackle the ambiguity, challenge, and change of this Decade of Disruption.

Wow! Championing innovation, challenging standard approaches, and taking risks – sounds scary, right?

Let's see how we can make it less so.

Experience and experiment

In a disruptive and ambiguous environment there are often more unknowns than knowns, and many of the challenges we face do not have clear solutions. Leadership experts Ron Heifetz and Marty Linsky refer to these kinds of challenges as 'adaptive' and suggest they have the following characteristics:

1. The problem is difficult to clearly define, and to do so may require learning, which means that…

2. The solution is currently unknown and will definitely require learning, which means that…

3. The work is achieved through innovation and influence rather than authority and power.

You can see that engaging in learning is essential to deal with the adaptive challenges that disruption inevitably throws our way – which is why it's such an important part of becoming antifragile.

Despite the discomfort involved, much of our learning comes from trial and error. As infants, we learn the basics of how to live by making many mistakes along the way – just think how many times a toddler falls down before learning how to walk! Being able to fail, and learn from failure, is an essential component of constructive learning. But it's something that many of us are not comfortable with. Harvard psychologist Tal Ben Shahar cites 'fear of failure, resulting from often unrealistic and perfectionist demands, as being one of the key detractors from learning, leading to lack of creativity and procrastination.'

The work of Professor Carol Dweck from Stanford University on growth and fixed mindsets provides insight as to why this is. Someone with a *fixed mindset* believes that things don't, won't, and can't change, including their skills, their talents, and their situation. They inherently believe 'I'm no good at public speaking', 'I'll never understand Excel spreadsheets', or 'I wasn't born with any musical talent.' They feel it is hopeless and pointless to even try to improve – so they don't.

Someone with a *growth mindset* understands that development is possible throughout our lives. They believe that effort, perseverance, and learning from mistakes are the root causes of success – not inherent ability or talent. Having a growth mindset is connected to better performance, better outcomes, greater perseverance in the face of challenge, and high levels of confidence and wellbeing in both children and adults.

However, in her book *Mindset: The New Psychology of Success*, Dweck makes the point that a growth mindset is not inherently 'good', just as a fixed mindset is not inherently 'bad'. The question to ask is: *Is my mindset helping or holding me back in this situation at this time?*

Whilst there are certain situations where a fixed mindset is preferable, a growth mindset is favoured when the answer is not clear, when we are feeling anxious, or when we've made a mistake or failed in some way. Does that sound familiar? Sounds to me like every day in this Decade of Disruption!

So how can we grow a growth mindset?

Let's be honest, it can be hard to engage a growth mindset when there's a lot going on or when you feel under pressure. It's at times like these that your brain's internal safety warning system sounds the alarm, telling you to play small and stay safe rather than take risks and learn. And that's just where the art of 'Tinkering' comes into play…

Tinkerbell is one of my favourite Disney characters. Notwithstanding the fact that she gets things wrong and loses her temper regularly, she is brave, loyal, funny, and not afraid to push boundaries. What I particularly like about Tinkerbell – and all the Tinker fairies – is their curiosity. When they look at something that's been thrown away – a 'Lost Thing' – they look at it with the question 'What's useful here? How could I use it in a different way? What can I reuse and recycle?'

As leaders, we could learn a lot from Tink. Tinkering is a valuable way to approach growing your growth mindset. Rather than pushing for big, bold steps, think about how you could 'Tinker' with what you already think, feel, and do, and what impact that might have.

To this end, I want to share with you a model I've used successfully with leaders and in my own leadering. Based on Kolb's reflective learning cycle and developed by my friends Michelle McQuaid and Beck Melville, the 'Learning Loop' uses the framework 'Act, Assess, Adjust' and can be used to grow your growth mindset in the work that you do every day.

The Learning Loop comprises three stages:

- **Act.** Experiment with new ways of thinking, feeling, or behaving that align with your goals.
- **Assess.** Review the feedback from your efforts and decide what is and isn't working.

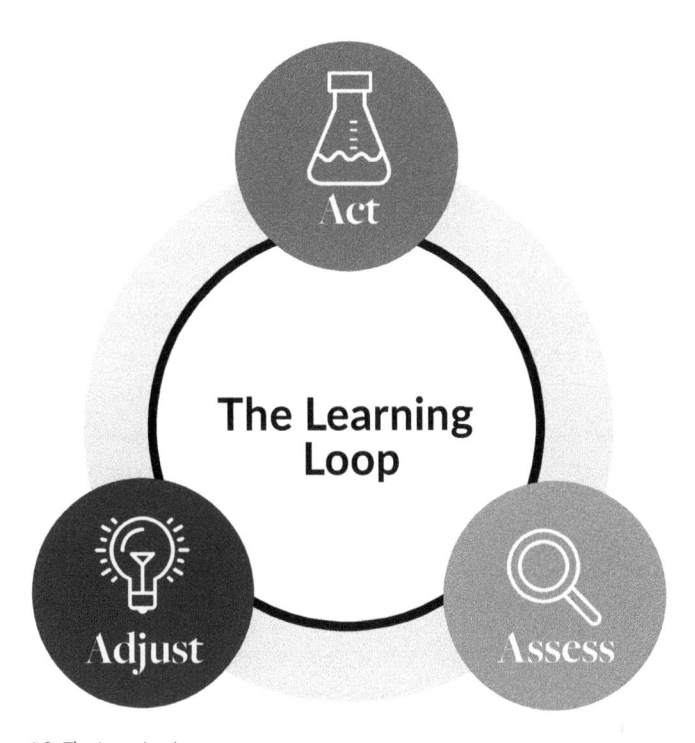

Figure 4.3: The Learning Loop

- **Adjust.** Look for ways to incorporate what you've learned into future actions and consider opportunities to try again.

The Learning Loop helps us in several ways. First, the Act stage is clearly action oriented, so it moves us from *thinking* about doing something differently to actually *doing* it. This also means that our learning is based on lived experience rather than just theorising about what could or might happen.

Second, the Assess stage keeps us curious and reflective so that we can assess the impact of our Tinkering. It's important at this stage not to let your inner critic take over. Asking *What went well? What did I learn?* can help you resist the urge to be judgemental and also provide a sense of achievement, which gives your brain a hit of the happy hormone dopamine and helps sustain your motivation to keep moving through the Loop.

Finally, the Adjust stage of the Learning Loop builds your capacity to try new things and increases your threshold for the perfectly imperfect nature of the real work that leaders have to do every day. This is particularly important in the ambiguous environment of the Decade of Disruption.

In order to build our capacities and achieve our goals, the Learning Loop must be repeated over and over to wire our neural pathways towards mastery. By keeping the risk small and adopting a Tinkering mindset, we keep our brains feeling safe, which boosts our motivation and confidence in trying something new. And that reduces our fragility.

> USE INTELLIGENT RISK HACK:
> **Be a Tinker.**
>
> *Ask: What can I play with in the Learning Loop today?*

Champion innovation

Did you know that vaccinations use a small dose or inactivated version of a disease to train your body to resist it in its stronger form? Or that by taking small doses of a poison, you can develop resistance to it? Well, it's true, and it's called *hormesis* – when negative actions actually protect you from something worse. In the same way, the art of Tinkering and living in the Learning Loop helps us resist leaning away from learning and become more immune to the 'poison' of risk. Hormesis in action!

Using these tools also helps build our capacity to feel comfortable with failure, and this is just what we need to encourage the innovation required to solve the adaptive challenges inherent in this Decade of Disruption. Embracing innovation is essential because, as we covered earlier, the knowledge doesn't yet exist to solve the challenges we're facing. But how do we do that? How do we make innovation 'happen'?

Well, contrary to what many people would have us believe, innovation can't be turned on and off, nor is it a 'strategy' that can be 'executed' through a plan. Famous innovations such as Post-its, Teflon, Viagra, and many others emerged out of experience, intuition, and experimentation – not from a strategic innovation process based on a specific plan. The insight needed for innovation doesn't come from a planning process; it comes from a combination of circumstance, desire, curiosity, and need. And it involves failing.

So rather than sponsoring an innovation 'strategy', we need to sponsor innovation by creating the *conditions* to innovate every day. And that means creating a sense of safety so that failure can be embraced rather than feared.

We all share the same deep psychological need to be seen, respected, and valued each day. Professor Amy Edmondson at Harvard Business School explains that psychological safety exists when we feel safe to take risks and be vulnerable by speaking up, offering new ideas, asking questions, valuing different opinions, and being willing and able to learn from our mistakes with the group. She suggests that psychological safety is 'not about being nice, it's about creating the space where honesty is truly possible' within teams.

When we do this, our clarity of thinking improves, we see differing views and conflict as productive rather than threatening, and we respond constructively to failure by discussing and learning from our mistakes rather than feeling embarrassed and avoiding them. When we feel challenged but not threatened, oxytocin levels in our brain go up, prompting feelings of trust and trust-making behaviour. We feel safe, so instead of focusing on self-protection, we focus on achieving shared goals and sharing novel ideas. In this kind of environment, innovation is a natural by-product.

Edmondson's research also found that leaders play a critical role in creating or killing psychological safety in teams. Whether a leader intentionally invites input, has necessary honest conversations quickly, owns their mistakes, shares what they're learning as they grow, and shows appreciation for other's questions and efforts, determines the level of psychological safety in a team.

Not surprisingly, an extensive two-year study at Google found that their highest-performing teams all had one thing in common – high levels of psychological safety.

So what does all this mean for becoming antifragile?

We need to create and maintain psychological safety for and within ourselves, without relying on others to do it for or with us. I call this *personal* psychological safety. When we do this, we can take that sense of safety with us wherever we go and draw on it whenever we need – it becomes portable. This *personal, portable* psychological safety enables us to apply Amy Edmondson's ideas to our own leadering by being curious, inviting feedback, and owning (and learning from) our mistakes. And when we do that, we'll feel safe enough to innovate and take the necessary intelligent risks to meet the challenges and opportunities in front of us.

As Professor B. J. Fogg, Founder of the Behavior Design Lab at Stanford University, suggests in his book *Tiny Habits*: 'Embrace mistakes and discoveries, and use them to move forward.'

> USE INTELLIGENT RISK HACK:
> **Create personal, portable psychological safety.**
> *Ask: What went well? Where did I struggle? What can I learn?*

Create antifragile optionality

In 2003, Barry Schwartz's book *The Paradox of Choice* was a *New York Times* bestseller. In it, Schwartz proposes that too much choice paralyses our capacity to decide. He identifies a tipping point after which more choice hinders rather than helps decision making. Multiple studies since have shown that an excess of choice often leads us to be less, not more, satisfied once we actually do decide. We're often left with a nagging feeling we could have done better. You know, the FOMO (fear of missing out) effect.

In terms of becoming antifragile, it's a similar picture. Having options to choose from means we don't have all our eggs in one basket, so when the inevitable disruption, challenge, and change come along, we're able to pivot to another option and either avoid negative impact or even benefit from the new environment. But if we are faced with too many options, we can feel overwhelmed.

That's why we shouldn't consider just *any* options. They need to be *smart* options, and this means two things:

1. Smart options are as independent of each other as possible. In other words, they each fail or succeed without impacting our

other options – there's no 'domino effect' or 'failure contagion' between them.

2. Smart options spread risk. In *Antifragile*, Taleb calls this the 'barbell strategy' because, like the weights on a barbell, you want your options to sit at either end of the risk spectrum. With some of your options you play it safe, which means you're robust if things take a turn for the worse. At the other end of the bar, you're taking lots of small risks – via the Learning Loop – so that you'll benefit if things go well.

Becoming antifragile means avoiding the middle of the bar – the 'moderate risk' zone – because, no matter how comfortable it may feel, it offers no great gain or loss. When you play in the middle, you can't benefit from the upside of disruption, and that makes you fragile. Remember, the antifragile test is that we get more upsides than downsides from uncertainty, challenge, and change. So what we are looking for are low-cost mistakes, with known maximum losses, and large, potentially boundless payoffs. Only then can you hope to benefit from more upsides than downsides in the Decade of Disruption.

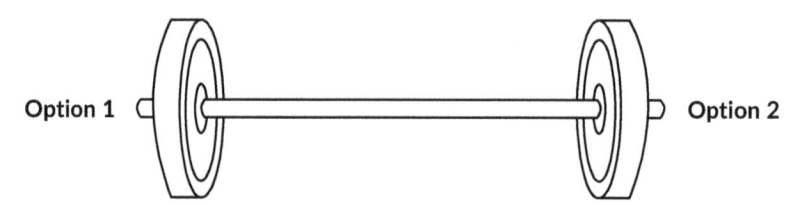

Option 1 ⬛━━━━━━━━━━━━━━━━━━⬛ **Option 2**

Figure 4.4: The optionality 'barbell' strategy

So, antifragile optionality is the combination of fierce confidence and a touch of paranoia – just enough to provide a safety net to protect yourself from extreme harm whilst letting the upsides take care of themselves. When we position ourselves in this way, we don't need to try to predict what's going to happen next (which in our complex environment is impossible anyway!). With antifragile optionality, our work is simply to evaluate the information available and to make a rational decision about the best option to follow on that basis.

GUIDING PRINCIPLES TO BECOMING ANTIFRAGILE

Here are some principles to guide your antifragile optionality:

1. Identify multiple options to achieve your desired outcomes.
2. Look for options with open-ended, potentially boundless, payoffs.
3. Rank outcomes according to their level of optionality – the more independent they are, the better.
4. Make like a barbell and stay away from the middle.

This quote from Taleb sums up the barbell strategy beautifully: 'So just as Stoicism is the domestication, not the elimination, of emotions, so is the barbell a domestication, not the elimination, of uncertainty.'

> USE INTELLIGENT RISK HACK:
> **Use the barbell strategy.**
> *Ask: What's my safety net? Where can I take a risk?*

PRINCIPLE 5: SEEK COLLECTIVE WISDOM

'It is said that the best horses lose when they compete with slower ones, and win against better rivals. Back the rider, not the horse.'
— NASSIM NICHOLAS TALEB

As a leader, it can feel like you have to shoulder all the responsibility, that it's your role to come up with a vision or a plan to solve problems. It can be difficult to acknowledge to yourself and others that you don't have all the answers. But it's an important step to take.

Antifragile leaders know they can't do it alone. When we put the principle of optionality into practice with our leading, we understand that we have a better chance of benefiting from the upside of disruption if we spread the leading load. We hold the tension and work from a space of not knowing whilst we intentionally seek collective wisdom, rather than taking control to facilitate action. We ask strategic questions, engage relevant stakeholders to help answer them, find people with the motivation and energy to take action, then quickly figure out together what's working and how it can be built upon.

When we operate in this way, we harness the benefit of respectful conflict between different perspectives, and we strengthen others by providing autonomy, making each person feel competent and confident in their capacity to contribute.

Harness the will

It's a well-known premise in business that competitive advantage lies in your people, not your product. In his book *The Infinite Game*, Simon Sinek talks about this in terms of 'will' versus 'resources'.

As a leader, the will you have available to harness lies with your people. Will is not about skills, knowledge, or experience, as important as these may be. Will is the energy, attitudes, and mindsets your people show up with each day. It's their motivation, commitment, and morale. It's intangible, but it's absolute gold. The will of your people drives their discretionary effort, problem solving, creativity, imagination, and teamwork.

Resources, on the other hand, are much easier to see, feel, and measure. They're the kinds of things you'd see on a performance dashboard or balance sheet – revenues, profit, production quotas, stock price, and so on. As leaders, it can be easy for us to focus on resources, as they are tangible and easily measured. This gives us – or rather our brains – a sense of control and a feeling of safety and security. But it's a false sense of security, and it make us fragile. The things that influence our capacity to accumulate resources are external and largely outside of our control – economic cycles, politics, major weather events, global pandemics. COVID-19 has shown us this all too clearly.

However, the factors that influence *will* lie with us and the way we lead our people. They are internally rather than externally driven. If we so choose, we can access and harness a bottomless pit of will by actively fostering trust and collaboration in our teams.

The good news is our brains are hardwired for connection, so we have both a biological and a psychological need for social support. Each time we genuinely connect with another person, the pleasure-inducing hormone oxytocin is released into our bloodstream, immediately reducing anxiety and improving concentration and focus. This is why employee satisfaction, retention, and productivity are higher among employees who report that their immediate boss cares about them – and so is profitability.

Studies have also found that having a sense of belonging is connected with a range of positive individual outcomes, including higher self-esteem, greater life satisfaction, faster recovery from disease, lower levels of stress, less mental illness, and longer lifespan.

The lesson from this? Becoming antifragile is not an individual sport! Invite others to join you.

> **SEEK COLLECTIVE WISDOM HACK:**
> **Share the load.**
>
> *Ask: How can I create opportunity for collaboration?*

Generate constructive conflict

It's no coincidence that we often have our biggest arguments with those we are closest to. Think about your brother, sister, cousin, or best friend. Recall the many differences of opinions that have been shared over a dinner table with family or close friends. The results can be explosive, but if we see them through a lens of curiosity rather than ego and a need to be right, we can gain valuable learning. In fact, very little learning comes from isolation. Throughout our childhood and adolescence, we not only create new learning through direct experiences or watching others, we also test and validate our thinking with people who may not have the same ideas or perspectives.

When we build learning communities like this in our teams, we reinforce learning outcomes, increase motivation and challenge, and generate more diverse ideas and solutions than when we operate alone. And this is particularly important when it comes to dealing with uncertainty, challenge, and change. Research suggests that our leadership approach is the number-one factor that impacts how successful we are in our responses to disruption and the wellbeing of the people involved.

In becoming antifragile, we are comfortable with respectful conflict and see disagreement as productive because we keep it focused on concepts and ideas. We recognise that it is essential for learning, development, and growth. We foster deep feelings of trust by expressing our own feelings and ideas in an appropriate and professional way, and encourage others to do the same. We do not avoid difficult conversations but have the courage to have the right conversation with the right person and provide constructive feedback focused on solving problems and removing obstacles. We see conflict not as a problem, but as a way for us to find the best possible solution in the shortest period of time.

> **SEEK COLLECTIVE WISDOM HACK:**
> **Look for the argument.**
>
> *Ask: Whom can I involve that has a different perspective?*

Let it go

In Part I, we showed that trying to predict the future based on what's happened in the past is unreliable for complex systems. When we truly take that on board, we understand what leadership writer Margaret Wheatley suggests – that trying to control disruption and what comes from it is a fool's errand. Once your mindset shifts to accept the inherent mess and magic in the natural way of life, it's easier to let go of what's not effective and embrace the things that can help ourselves and others take on new perspectives and ways of doing things. This is how we thrive in the Decade of Disruption.

Leadership and organisational development researcher Gervase Bushe has spent over three decades transforming organisational structures, cultures, and processes away from command and control and towards more collaborative work systems. He suggests that instead of trying to 'manage change' as a response to disruption, we should instead look for ways to coach people to create positive changes. We can do this by 'tracking' – actively looking for the things we want more of and recognising where and why they are occurring – and 'fanning' – adding resources and support, and acknowledging and appreciating people's efforts in order to heighten energy, momentum, and commitment.

As we become antifragile we let go of the illusion of control, honour people's energy, and give them the autonomy and opportunities to self-organise around actions that matter to them.

> **SEEK COLLECTIVE WISDOM HACK:**
> **Track and fan.**
>
> *Ask: How can I 'track' the energy and 'fan' the flames?*

PRINCIPLE 6: TACKLE THE INFINITE GAME

We are all playing games. It's the *type* of game we play that determines how we engage with life and leadering. Professor James P. Carse first proposed the idea of the infinite game in his 1987 book, *Finite and Infinite Games: A Vision of Life as Play and Possibility*. He suggests that finite games are inherently competitive, bounded by rules, fuelled by power, and 'theatrical' in the sense that there are players on the field and spectators in the stands. Perhaps most importantly, finite games have an endpoint: a time at which there is a 'winner' and a 'loser'. By contrast, the infinite game (and there is only one) exists solely for the purpose of continuing the game. When we play the infinite game, there are boundaries rather than rules, participants rather than players and spectators, and self-sustaining strengths rather than power play and politics.

Playing the infinite game in the Decade of Disruption requires a change in perspective: we must understand that we only compete with ourselves, not others; that the only success is not to win but to continue playing; and that to create the conditions to do so, we must collaborate with others. The infinite game goes beyond short term versus long term. To quote Simon Sinek, the infinite game 'is not about the next quarter or the next election; it is about the next generation.'

When we play the infinite game we play *with* the rules rather than by them. The players, playing time, rules, playing field, and possible outcomes are not prescribed or fixed. Changing any one of these elements does not change the game, so change is not seen as a source of disruption or something to be avoided or feared. Rather, it is accepted as an inherent part of the game and so we remain open to the possibilities it presents.

Change is accepted as an inherent part of the infinite game and so we remain open to the possibilities it presents.

Walt Disney was playing the infinite game when he set up Disneyland. 'Disneyland will never be finished,' he explained. 'It's something we can keep developing and adding to. A motion picture is different.

Once it's wrapped up and sent out for processing, we're through with it. If there are things that could be improved, we can't do anything about them anymore. I've always wanted to work on something alive, something that keeps growing. We've got that in Disneyland'.

When we play the infinite game:

- Rather than winning the game, our goal is to keep the game going and keep playing.

- Rather than looking to bring the game to a conclusion, we facilitate the game and help to sustain it, to make it thrive and prosper.

- Rather than playing to protect, gain, or expand power, we play to our limitless strengths – our own and others', in combination and collectively – to achieve outcomes that may be felt beyond our time playing.

By showing the ability to create potential and possibilities, the players of the infinite game improve their chances of attracting other players and support the infinite game itself. This is why playing the infinite game makes us antifragile: it allows us to draw on collective wisdom, leverage optionality, and learn from the many diverse participants.

As leaders, we need to understand and accept that in the Decade of Disruption, finite games are increasingly irrelevant. As we deal with ever more ambiguous and adaptive challenges in an ever more complex and interdependent world, the idea that we should compete to succeed is ludicrous. Winning becomes irrelevant because by the time we reach the level of mastery necessary to win, the game has changed. Playing to win is a zero-sum game.

In playing the infinite game we need to adapt, pivot, be agile, have options, and play with boundaries rather than within them. Only by playing the infinite game can we benefit from the upsides of disruption, uncertainty, and change. And that's how we become antifragile.

> **TACKLE THE INFINITE GAME HACK:**
> **Reject zero-sum.**
>
> *Ask: How can I play the infinite game today?*

ROBUST PRINCIPLES: THE BECOMING ANTIFRAGILE TRAVEL GUIDE

I don't know about you, but when I'm travelling somewhere I've never been I like to have some understanding of how things work there before I leave. Things like the currency, the language, the main modes of transport, the cultural customs, and so on. It makes the journey a lot easier and means I can gain more from my experiences because I've got some guiding principles under my belt before I arrive to help me navigate the physical, economic, and cultural landscape.

You can think of the ROBUST principles in the same way. They are your Lonely Planet Guide to becoming antifragile. They don't tell you the specific landmarks you might want to visit or where you should focus your time and energy, but they give you a clear idea of what's available to help you make the most of your journey and the experience.

I know we've covered a lot of information, so here's a brief summary of the hacks for each of the ROBUST principles.

Recruit the Brain	Operate in Reality	Break the Negative/Build the Positive	Use Intelligent Risk	Seek Collective Wisdom	Tackle the Infinite Game
Challenge your negativity bias. Ask: What's going well or working well here?	**Be a control freak.** Ask: What can't I control? What can I control? What can I influence?	**Create a 'not to do' list.** Ask: What am I not going to do?	**Be a Tinker.** Ask: What can I play with in the Learning Loop today?	**Share the load.** Ask: How can I create opportunity for collaboration?	**Reject zero-sum.** Ask: How can I play the infinite game today?
Know what you want. Ask: What do I want more of in my life? What do I want to work towards?	**Find the fairy tale.** Ask: Is it true? Can I absolutely know that it is true? Who am I when I believe that story? Who would I be without it?	**Have an anti-role model.** Ask: What kind of leader do I not want to be?	**Create personal, portable psychological safety.** Ask: What went well? Where did I struggle? What can I learn?	**Generate constructive conflict.** Ask: Who can I involve that has a different perspective on this?	
Be a stress detective. Ask: What am I feeling and where?	**Be mindful.** Ask: Why am I here? Where is my focus? How am I showing up?	**Nurture your inner optimist.** Ask: What's the best I can hope for given what I know?	**Use the barbell strategy.** Ask: What's my safety net? Where can I take a risk?	**Track and fan.** Ask: How can I 'track' the energy and 'fan' the flames?	
		Leverage your strengths. Ask: How can I use my strengths to meet this challenge?			

Figure 4.5: ROBUST principles

SUMMARY

» *In the volatile, uncertain, complex, and ambiguous (VUCA) environment of the Decade of Disruption, we need to let go of the idea that we can control change through strategy, planning, and rules.*

» *Heuristics provide rules of thumb that are imperfect but make things simple and easier to implement. They are flexible and expansive, meet the demands of a complex and changing environment, and reveal a clear pathway forward.*

» *The six ROBUST principles are guiding heuristics that can be applied across a range of contexts in your personal and professional life to help you become antifragile.*

» *Each ROBUST principle has a series of hacks in the form of a question or questions that encourage you to be curious and reflective and get to the heart of the work that needs to be done. These are summarised in the preceding table.*

REFERENCES

All Nassim Nicholas Taleb quotes... Taleb, N. N. (2013). *Antifragile: Things That Gain from Disorder.* London, UK: Penguin.

it has been shown that negativity bias reduces life satisfaction and increases anxiety and depression... Williams, L. M., Gatt, J. M., Schofield, P. R., Olivieri, G., Peduto, A., & Gordon, E. (2009). 'Negativity bias' in risk for depression and anxiety: Brain–body fear circuitry correlates, 5-HTT-LPR and early life stress. *Neuroimage, 47*(3), 804–814.

we can only consciously process around 40... Wilson, T. (2004). *Strangers to Ourselves: Discovering the Adaptive Unconscious.* Belknap Press.

Workplace drama researcher Cy Wakeman... Wakeman, C. (2017, October 18). A "drama researcher" explains how to avoid drama at work. Quartz at Work. Retrieved from https://qz.com/work/1101863/a-psychologist-explains-how-to-stop-wasting-time-on-work-drama/

Whilst some of these stories are accurate, many are not... Seligman, M. E. P (1990). *Learned Optimism: How to Change Your Mind and Your Life.* New York, NY: **Vintage Books**

and so it is just one of millions of possibilities that could be constructed in any given second Zimmerman, M. (1986). "Neurophysiology of Sensory Systems." In: Robert F. Schmidt (Ed.), *Fundamentals of Sensory Physiology.* Springer-Verlag: Berlin.

Studies have shown that performance deteriorates significantly as soon as we attempt more than one cognitive task at a time... Rock, D (2009). *Your Brain at Work: Strategies for Overcoming Distraction, Regaining Focus, and Working Smarter All Day Long.* New York, NY: Harper Collins

Multitasking diffuses attention, compromises memory, and can impede performance... Rock, D (2009). *Your Brain at Work: Strategies for Overcoming Distraction, Regaining Focus, and Working Smarter All Day Long.* New York, NY: Harper Collins

It can take up to 15 minutes to restore concentration following a distraction due to a refractory period in the brain... Rock, D (2009). *Your Brain at Work: Strategies for Overcoming Distraction, Regaining Focus, and Working Smarter All Day Long.* New York, NY: Harper Collins

Increases the amount of time necessary to finish the primary task by as much as 25%... Rock, D (2009). *Your Brain at Work: Strategies for Overcoming Distraction, Regaining Focus, and Working Smarter All Day Long.* New York, NY: Harper Collins

mindfulness practice improves both creativity and problem-solving skills... Rieken, B., Shapiro, S., Gilmartin, S., & Sheppard, S. D. (2019, January 4). How mindfulness can help engineers solve problems. *Harvard Business Review*.

The great German algebraist Carl Jacobi said... https://fs.blog/2013/10/inversion/

Particularly relevant to becoming antifragile is realistic, flexible optimism... Schneider, S. L. (2001). In search of realistic optimism. Meaning, knowledge, and warm fuzziness. J Am Psychol. 56(3): 250–63.

Research suggests that, in most workplaces, we spend around 80% of our time talking about problems and just 20% discussing what's working well... Cooperrider, D. L., & Godwin, L. (2011). Positive organization development: Innovation-inspired change in an economy and ecology of strengths. In: *Oxford Handbook of Positive Organizational Scholarship*, 737–50.

All the evidence suggests that we get to our highest performance by building strengths rather than fixing weaknesses... McQuaid, M., & Lawn, E. (2014). *Your Strengths Blueprint: How to be Engaged, Energized and Happy at Work.* Albert Park: VIC. Michelle McQuaid P/L

Studies show that people who use their strengths regularly are less stressed, more confident, happier, more energetic, and more satisfied, engaged, and creative at work... McQuaid, M., & Lawn, E. (2014). *Your Strengths Blueprint: How to be Engaged, Energized and Happy at Work.* Albert Park: VIC. Michelle McQuaid P/L

researchers recommend that we flip the 80:20 ratio to spend at least 80% of your time building on your strengths... Cooperrider, D. L., & McQuaid, M. (2012). "The positive arc of systemic strengths: How appreciative inquiry and sustainable designing can bring out the best in human systems". *The Journal of Corporate Citizenship*, 46, The Positive Psychology of Sustainable Enterprise (Summer 2012), pp. 71–102

But research has found the leaders who champion innovation, challenge standard approaches, and lead change are rated significantly more positively by their teams, peers, and bosses in terms of their leadership effectiveness... https://www.forbes.com/sites/joefolkman/2019/02/12/how-self-confidence-can-help-or-hurt-leaders/#4c1f7af59908

Leadership experts Ron Heifetz and Marty Linsky refer to these kinds of challenges as 'adaptive'... Heifetz, R., & Linsky, M. (2002, June). A survival guide for leaders. *Harvard Business Review.*

leading to lack of creativity and procrastination... Shahar, T. B. (2010). Learn to fail or fail to learn. Presented at The Mind and Its Potential Conference, Sydney, Australia, 2010.

Having a growth mindset is connected to better performance, better outcomes, greater perseverance in the face of challenge, and high levels of confidence and wellbeing in both children and adults... Dweck, C. (2006). *Mindset: The New Psychology of Success.* New York, NY: Random House.

Based on Kolb's (1984) reflective learning cycle... Kolb, D. (1984). *Experiential Learning: Experience as the Source of Learning and Development.* Englewood Cliffs, Prentice Hall.

Edmondson's research also found that leaders play a critical role in creating or killing psychological safety in teams ... Edmondson, A. (2012). *Teaming: How Organizations Learn, Innovate, and Compete in the Knowledge Economy.* John Wiley & sons: San Francisco.

an extensive two-year study at Google found that their highest-performing teams all had one thing in common – high levels of psychological safety... Delizonna, L. (2017). High-performing teams need psychological safety. Here's how to create it. *Harvard Business Review,* 8: 1–5.

Multiple studies since have shown that an excess of choice often leads us to be less, not more, satisfied once we actually do decide... https://procrastination.com/blog/9/decision-paralysis-overthinking-choices

employee satisfaction, retention, and productivity are higher among employees who report that their immediate boss cares about them... Rath, T. Harter, J.K. & Harter, K. (2010). *Wellbeing: The Five Essential Pillars.* New York, NY: Simon and Schuster.

having a sense of belonging is connected with a range of positive individual outcomes... Smith, E. E. (2017). *The Power of Meaning: Crafting a Life that Matters.* New York, NY: Random House

Research suggests that leadership approach is the number-one factor that impacts how successful we are in our responses to disruption and the wellbeing

of the people involved... The Change Lab 2019 Workplace Survey https://www.michellemcquaid.com/product/change-lab-2019-workplace-survey/

Margaret Wheatley suggests that trying to control disruption and what comes from it is a fool's errand... Wheatley, M. J. (2017) *Who Do We Choose To Be? Facing Reality, Claiming Leadership, Restoring Sanity*. San Francisco, CA. Berrett-Koehler

Gervase suggests that instead of trying to 'manage change' as a response to disruption, leaders should instead look for ways to coach people to create positive changes... Bushe, G. R., & Marshak, R. J. (2016). The Dialogic Mindset: Leading Emergent Change in a Complex World. *Organization Development Journal*, 37–65.

actively looking for the things we want more of and recognising where and why they are occurring... Bushe, G. R., & Marshak, R. J. (2016). The Dialogic Mindset: Leading Emergent Change in a Complex World. *Organization Development Journal*, 37–65.

To quote Simon Sinek the infinite game 'is not about the next quarter or the next election; it is about the next generation.'... Sinek, S. (2019). *The Infinite Game*. New York: Random House, p. xiii.

Disneyland will never be finished... Gabler, Neil (2007). *Walt Disney: The Triumph of American Imagination*. New York: Vintage.

LUNCH AND LEARN

Glenn guided Alex to a corner table on the café terrace, away from the noise and conversation of people enjoying lunch. This was an important conversation that needed space and privacy. The last few weeks on the project had not gone well: the client was more concerned about deliverables than ever, and Alex's team seemed to be imploding – a few of them had been in touch with HR about the stress and dysfunction in the team. Glenn needed to hear what was going on from Alex's perspective, and for them to find a way forward together. She needed to let Alex know her concerns without making it feel like a reprimand, and she had a feeling it wasn't going to be easy.

An hour later, Glenn had a clearer idea of what was happening. Alex had shared how much time, effort, and energy was going into listening to the team's complaints about the challenges of the project, the client, and each other. How the open-door leadership style recommended as part of the company's in-house leadership program left little time to get work done, or to think and plan. How depleted, demoralised, and dejected Alex was feeling about the project, the team, and the future.

Glenn could see that Alex was trying hard and had good intentions but had a scattered and inconsistent approach to leading the project and the team. Alex was lacking a set of guiding principles – a solid foundation that could foster a consistent, strategic approach and reduce the drain on everyone's emotional energy. Glenn shared a few principles that she used in her own leadership to help Alex begin to get things back on track, but she could see that replenishing energy, rebuilding positive attitudes, and shifting Alex's leadership mindset for the long term was not going to be a quick fix.

GUIDING PRINCIPLES TO BECOMING ANTIFRAGILE

WHAT DO YOU SEE?

- Alex needs some ideas – based on the information Glenn shares, what two ROBUST principles do you think would help Alex the most?

- Which of the ROBUST 'hacks' do you already use regularly?

- Which hacks do you think will be most useful on your journey to becoming antifragile?

PART III

HOW TO DO IT... EVERY DAY

Okay, let's check in. By this stage you know why you need to go on the journey, and you've scoped the landscape, opened the map, and got the travel guide. Now it's time to create your personalised route to becoming antifragile. In this section we look at what it means to have Antifragile Energy, Antifragile Attitudes, and Antifragile Mindsets, and how these can make a difference in your life and leadering. By the end of this section, you'll understand what the first steps of your Becoming Antifragile journey could look like.

THE BUILDING BLOCKS OF BECOMING ANTIFRAGILE

Our Energy, Attitudes, and Mindsets are the building blocks of becoming antifragile because they shape how we see and show up in the world through our thoughts, feelings, and behaviours. Antifragile Energy, Attitudes, and Mindsets leverage our leading capacity and capability to magnify the impact and outcomes of our efforts.

Antifragile Energy

Antifragile Energy is renewable and sustainable. It is not finite; its creation does not sap energy from others. Rather, it has a multiplier effect: it creates energy for us and others. Antifragile Energy is broad and deep, as it comes from multiple sources: physical, mental, and emotional.

Physical energy is our foundation, as we sustain our bodies and minds through nutrition, sleep, movement, and rest.

Mental energy – perhaps our most precious resource – helps us focus, grapple with complexity, and make good decisions.

Emotional energy enables us to understand how to harness and ride the natural highs and lows of life by limiting self-sabotage and reconnecting with the simple pleasures that sustain us, even in the face of external pressures.

Renewable and sustainable, energy blended from these three sources makes us less fragile; enhances our ability to deal with disruption, challenge, and change; and fuels our journey to Becoming AntiFragile.

Antifragile Attitudes

Antifragile Attitudes help us be courageous as we engage with the world. They support us to feel confident to take on challenging tasks, to stand by our point of view without arrogance, to make tough decisions when needed, and to put in the necessary effort to succeed.

GUIDING PRINCIPLES TO BECOMING ANTIFRAGILE

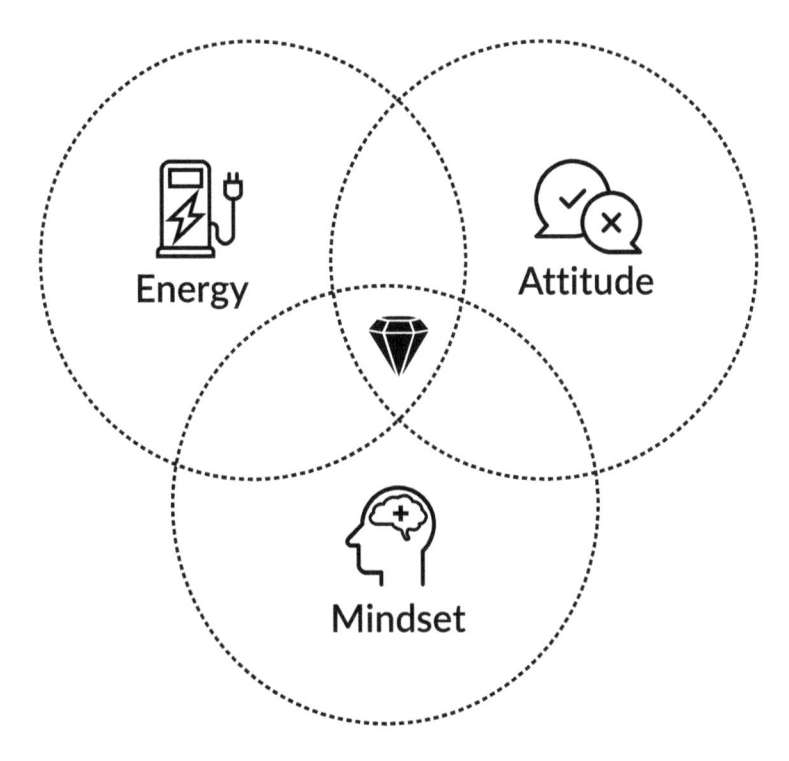

Figure III: The building blocks of Becoming Antifragile: Energy, Attitudes, and Mindsets

Antifragile Attitudes keep us motivated, committed, and action oriented. With positive expectations about succeeding now and in the future, we accept the inherent complexity and natural ups and downs of life and persevere towards our goals. When necessary, we are agile and fluid and redirect our action pathways.

Committed to making purposeful progress, we intentionally focus on the best contribution that we can make and empower others to do the same. We are daring enough to take acceptable risks in the name of progress and to be vulnerable when we are challenged or fail so that we can reach out for help and support.

Antifragile Mindsets

Antifragile Mindsets set our agenda and help us to deal with pressure, complexity, and the unexpected. They define the guiding principles for our work and provide the guiding light for our journey. When we are faced with disruption, challenge, and change it is natural to want to stay safe – to fear failure, to avoid risk, and to feel a fragile sense of competence and self-belief.

When we have Antifragile Mindsets, we accept the inevitability of change, let go of the need for control, and are flexible in our position and perspective. We are agile – growing and learning from experience, both good and bad. We take on board diverse perspectives that challenge our own, we are curious, we encourage experimentation, and we make the most of learning opportunities embedded in responsible failure. When we do fail, we are self-aware, able to reflect on our actions from an impersonal, strategic perspective and to act, assess, and adjust accordingly so that we keep putting our new learning into action in the world.

With Antifragile Mindsets, we play the infinite game with a vision for contribution and the greater good, which takes us beyond ego to have a bigger impact in the world – beyond ourselves and beyond our lifetime.

5.

RENEWABLE ANTIFRAGILE ENERGY

ENERGY IS THE LEVERAGE POINT IN THE TIME-EFFORT-ENERGY EQUAtion. We can't create more time, and effort is dependent to a great extent on the energy we have available – so it makes sense that we focus our efforts on creating multiple, abundant, renewable sources of energy to draw from.

But that's not what we're doing. Research has found that most of us are struggling to maintain our energy levels on a daily basis. For example, in one study more than 10,000 participants were asked to rate their energy levels for the previous day, and only 11% said they had a great deal of energy. We have an energy crisis on our hands.

The essence of energy

A physics textbook will tell you that energy is 'the capacity to do work' and that work is 'the action of moving something against a force'. Mmmmm, that doesn't give us much to work with, does it? It's like defining a rainbow as 'light refracted through water' – you can't argue with it, but it doesn't really satisfy.

The reason energy is so hard to define is because it's an abstract concept. There is no physical 'essence' of energy, and no such thing as 'pure energy'. Energy is always carried *by* something, usually in the form of movement. So, for example, kinetic energy is carried by a billiard ball rolling across a table – the heavier the ball is, the more energy it carries. Personal energy is much the same. You can't see it, but you know when it's there and you definitely know when it's missing – when you feel stuck, a bit lost, unable to get moving.

> *We need energy to engage with life and ultimately to thrive.*

Let's use the basic idea of energy as 'the capacity to do work that causes movement', and define that movement as becoming antifragile. We need energy in order to do the work needed to become antifragile, and if we apply the ROBUST principles to generate that energy, we'll be using Antifragile Energy to become antifragile – win-win!

Just as there are different forms of energy that cause movement in physics, there are different forms of energy that we can use to fuel our movement through life. Some energy is generated within us and fuels our motivation and engagement. We might call this 'personal energy' – things like how we are feeling physically, how focused and mentally alert we are, and how we are feeling emotionally – happy, sad, confident, anxious. Personal energy, then, falls into three categories:

1. Physical
2. Emotional
3. Mental.

> *Personal energy is like a three-legged stool – if one of the legs is out of balance, the whole stool can tip over.*

Are we tired or invigorated, hungry or satisfied, sad or happy, relaxed or stressed? While these things may be impacted by factors outside ourselves, ultimately they are about how we feel personally, as an individual. And we need all three to feel well, do well, and lead well.

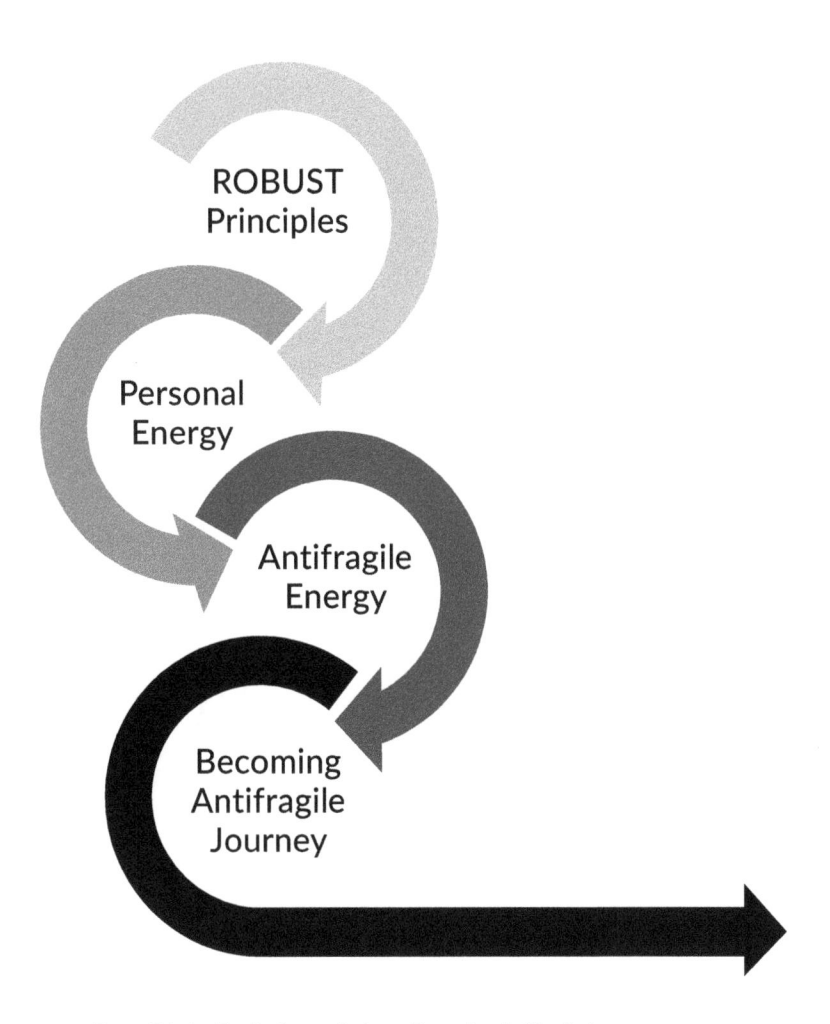

Figure 5.1: Antifragile Energy fuels our Becoming Antifragile journey.

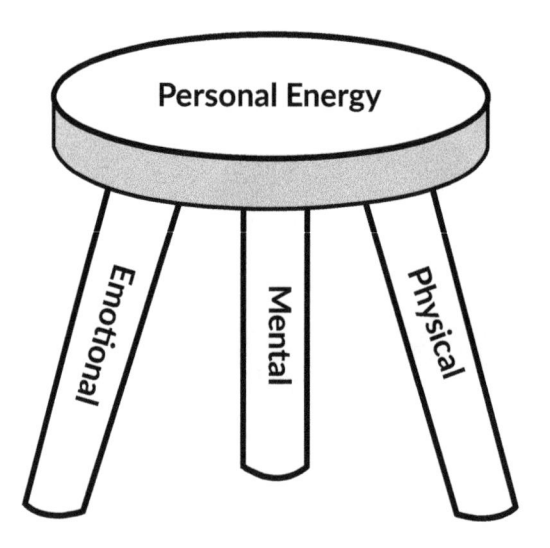

Figure 5.2: The three-legged stool of Personal Energy

The particular 'blend' of physical, mental, and emotional fuel required to provide the personal energy to get moving will vary for different people and in different contexts and situations. What you need at work will be different than at home, and what works for you now may not work later today, next week, or further into the future.

To understand more, let's dive deeper into each energy source.

PHYSICAL ENERGY

The sheer amount of information available about how we should look after our bodies can be overwhelming. Add to that the fact that much of it is competing, contradictory, or constantly changing, and it's easy to put it in the 'too hard' basket. It's just too much effort to work out what advice to follow. It can also be easy to fall into the 'I'm too busy' trap.

Maximising energy doesn't mean you need to be a perfect physical specimen and live a perfect life. It's important to recognise – and accept – that when it comes to physical energy, each of us is starting from a different place. The important thing is that you are willing to take action (remember the 'Act' of the Learning Loop?) and start Tinkering ('Assess' and 'Adjust') with ways to make the best of what is available to you.

Small choices about how you rest, move, and eat can have a much bigger impact on your levels of physical energy than you might expect.

Physical energy is essential to becoming antifragile. But our bodies aren't machines. They don't run at a steady, consistent pace throughout the day from the moment we wake until the moment we go to bed. Like every other living creature on this planet, our energy moves in waves. We expend energy, then we need to rest and refuel in order to continue to thrive throughout the day.

Unfortunately, research shows that, on the whole, we are pretty bad judges of just how important looking after our body is to our confidence, ability, and motivation to thrive through disruption. So let's look at the three main ways we can increase our physical energy.

1. Refuel – Make smart food choices

There's so much information out there about food and diet, this whole book could be dedicated to it. Personally, I love Michael Pollan's book *Food Rules*. Working with the overarching premise of 'Eat food. Mostly plants. Not too much', he suggests several principles we can apply to make good nutritional choices. My personal favourites are 'Don't eat food that your great grandmother wouldn't recognise' and 'Don't buy food where you buy your petrol.' Good advice indeed!

On a more tactical level, as you go through the day and think about your food choices, be smart and strategic. Ask yourself, *What kind of energy do I need for the next few hours?* and consider whether what you're about to eat is going to help you generate that energy. Take your own food into the office so that you're not tempted by easy but unhealthy takeaway options when you're hungry and time-poor. If you keep servings small and indulgences rare (pick the moments you can afford the energy slumps), you're likely to have less guilt, more enjoyment, better health, and more energy.

When it comes to refuelling your body, when you eat can be as critical as what you eat.

But it's not just about what you eat. It's also important to be mindful of *when* you eat. How often have you left it so late to eat that by the time you're deciding what to put on the plate, you're time-poor and your energy levels have already hit rock bottom? I know I have! At that point I want foods that are easy, and that will give me a quick energy hit – and/or comfort me if I'm feeling tired or stressed (or both!). But of course, what the mind craves in these moments of weakness is not what the body needs. Studies have found that consistently choosing to eat wisely in terms of what we eat and when not only improves our immediate energy levels, but can also lift our mood and bolster our short- and long-term health.

2. Rest – Create space

Research suggests about 95 percent of us need somewhere between seven and nine hours of sleep per night, with a few of us needing a little more or less. Unfortunately, roughly two-thirds of us report that we don't get enough sleep. As a result, not only do we struggle to maximise our energy, but we also suffer negative impacts on our health, mood, mental capacity, and productivity.

For example, some studies have found that losing ninety minutes of sleep can reduce daytime alertness by nearly one-third and that four hours of sleep loss produces the same level of impairment as drinking a six-pack of beer before work. So the next time you think that just one more hour working on that project or catching up with friends won't make that much difference, you might want to think again.

What can you do to encourage a restful night's sleep? Go to bed and wake up at the same time each day. Get rid of anything in your bedroom that might distract you from sleep, such as noises, bright lights, an uncomfortable bed, or a TV or computer. Keep the temperature in your bedroom on the cool side. And if you find yourself still awake after lying in bed for more than 20 minutes, get up and do a relaxing activity until you feel sleepy. The anxiety of not being able to sleep will only make getting there even harder!

Make time to rest and unwind as part of your daily routine.

Of course, giving your body time to rest shouldn't only happen at night. It's important to find time to rest during the day as well. Set aside time to unwind. Make a relaxing activity, such as reading or listening to music, part of your daily routine – even if only for 10 minutes.

3. Rouse – Become passively active

Did you know that physical activity releases soothing neuro- transmitters that help your brain to learn and grow, improve your mood, and help you to sleep and function better? So whilst you may think you're being more productive by sitting at your desk for longer, you can maximise your energy by making time for regular movement throughout the day.

Keeping physically active helps to generate mental, emotional, and relational energy.

You can break out of the 'I'm too busy' trap and become 'passively active' by building activity into your day. For example, if you have to sit for several hours a day at work, set a timer and break it up – even 2 minutes of leisurely walking every 60–90 minutes is enough to stabilise your blood sugar levels. If possible, get a standing desk extension so you can choose to stand and work when you want to, and take walking meetings whenever practical. I guarantee you'll feel the benefit – taking regular breaks has been found to improve both creativity and productivity.

EMOTIONAL ENERGY

How are you?

It's one of the most common questions we ask and are asked, but how often, I wonder, do we really know the answer to it? How often are we really aware of what we're feeling?

Emotions are powerful, abstract states of mind that influence how we think, what we pay attention to, our identity and self-concept, our evaluations of the world, what we consider important and valuable, how we make decisions, and our personal and professional relationships. You've probably heard of Emotional Intelligence. Widely recognised as being critical to effective leadership, it is the capacity to *be aware of*, *control*, and *express* one's emotions, and to handle interpersonal relationships thoughtfully and empathetically.

But what about the capacity to generate energy by *experiencing*, *expressing*, and intentionally *encouraging* positive emotions? Is that part of your leadership development plan? Well, maybe it should be.

Positive emotions have been found to produce success in life as much as they reflect it.

Research has found that our levels of positive emotions impact outcomes at every level of our lives: physical outcomes, such as immune function; work outcomes, such as productivity and absenteeism; social outcomes, such as quality of social interactions and relationships; personal outcomes, such as creativity and energy; and a range of psychological outcomes, such as resilience, self-confidence, and self-regulation.

Professor Barbara Fredrickson has found that positive emotions help to broaden and build the way our brains respond to opportunities and challenges. Her work suggests that experiencing emotions such as joy, pride, gratitude, amusement, interest, awe, inspiration, hope, love, and serenity can make us more optimistic, resilient, open, accepting, and driven by purpose.

Studies have repeatedly shown that experiencing positive emotions broadens our thinking and attention, builds our psychological and social resources, enhances resilience, reverses the impact of negative emotions, and triggers upward spirals of connection, collaboration, and performance. For example, when you are in a neutral or negative mood you see about 15% of what's happening around you through your peripheral vision. But when you're in a positive mood this expands to about 75% – an increase of over 400%!

You are also often able to think more quickly and creatively when you're in a positive mood because your brain is flooded with the feel-good neurotransmitters dopamine and serotonin. And, because your brain feels safe, you're also more likely to connect with others easily and think a little less about 'me' and a little more about 'we'. The great thing is, positive emotions don't just give us an advantage in the moment. As your feel-good experiences build up over time, they create a reserve – a bit like savings in your bank account – that helps you to thrive even in challenging times.

Now that sounds a bit like becoming antifragile, doesn't it?

> The foundation for a happy life is to accept the full range of our emotions – both positive and painful – by allowing them to flow through us.

'But what about the other end of the spectrum?' I hear you ask. 'It's not realistic to be positive all the time.' Well, you're absolutely right. It is equally important to accept and create space in our lives for negative emotions as an integral part of life's full experience. We must give ourselves permission to be human.

Fredrickson's work found that people who consistently thrive experience both positive and painful emotions. She suggests these emotions work like the balance between levity and gravity. Too many positive emotions – too much levity – and we risk floating away and becoming disconnected from reality. But too many painful, negative emotions – too much gravity – can de-energise us and leave us unable to create movement.

Rather than ignoring, suppressing, or distracting ourselves from the discomfort of painful, negative emotions, a more helpful way to engage with them is to see them as valuable learning and growth opportunities. For example, feelings of guilt can make you aware of the hurt you have caused someone and motivate you to be more socially sensitive and caring. Feelings of anger can give you the energy to take meaningful action.

Dr Robert Biswas-Diener suggests that rather than fearing negative emotions because they are painful and uncomfortable, we should think about emotions such as fear, anger, or anxiety simply as feedback and information from our body's internal security system – an alert that there is something important we need to know to keep us safe or to help us learn and grow.

But in terms of your Becoming Antifragile journey, intentionally generating more positive emotional experiences than negative ones is a sure-fire way to generate positive energy to fuel your journey to becoming antifragile.

Figure 5.3: Positive emotions create a reserve, like savings in a piggy bank.

Look for the positive

It may have come as no surprise to you that experiencing positive emotions helps us to thrive. However, it's not just about the overall volume of emotions we experience. Research also highlights the importance of frequency – that is, having these experiences regularly and often. By way of analogy, you'll feel better after six small meals than you will after one big dinner.

> **We need to intentionally look for and prioritise opportunities for small 'jolts of joy' every day.**

And rather than seeing these moments as icing on the cake of life, we need to see them as an essential ingredient of the cake itself. We need to move them from a 'nice to have' to a 'need to have'.

Even in the most challenging situations there is still goodness to be found. Very rarely is anything or anyone 100% good or bad; in every person and situation there is a mixture of both positive and negative attributes. Often, however, the negativity bias of our brains means it's the negative side of things that gets the most attention. Using the *Recruit the Brain* and *Build the Positive* ROBUST principles means finding ways to notice, look for, and then amplify the positive, which can help prevent negativity from taking over your experience.

Checking in on where you're at increases self-awareness of your emotions and can help you recognise where you might need to make some adjustments to dial up your positivity and dial down your negativity. Deliberately seek out, register, and amplify the good things in life. Look for patterns; try to understand what brings different positive emotions into your life – what gives you a jolt of joy – and do it more often. In this way, you'll build your personal positivity toolkit, which will be a valuable resource to draw on in challenging times.

Figure 5.4: We need to strike a balance in our levels of positivity between levity and gravity.

MENTAL ENERGY

Multitasking requires 'switching time', which increases the time needed to finish the primary task by as much as 25% and drains mental energy.

In 2014, social networking company The Draugiem Group used a time-tracking productivity app to study what habits set their most productive employees apart. Surprisingly, the 10% of employees with the highest productivity didn't put in longer hours than anyone else – often they didn't even work full 8-hour days. Rather, the key to their productivity was that for every 52 minutes of focused work, they took a 17-minute break.

There are biological limits that underlie mental performance. As we covered in the *Recruit the Brain* ROBUST principle, the brain is not designed for multitasking. Even the brain of a PhD is reduced to that of an 8-year-old when trying to do two things at once. A temporary shift in attention from one task to another – stopping to answer an e-mail or take a phone call — increases the amount of time necessary to finish the primary task as your brain switches from one task to another.

In Chapter 3 you learned a little about the prefrontal cortex (PFC) of your brain. Comprising only about 4–5% of the brain's volume, the PFC sits just behind the forehead and was the last region of the brain to evolve. The PFC is where intentional action is designed, developed, and decided upon through five functions: understanding, deciding, recalling, memorising, and inhibiting. These five individual functions combine for us to perform what are known as 'executive functions': things like planning, goal setting, problem solving, communicating, controlling impulses, and so on. The PFC is also our internal radio – a constant commentary making sense of the external world we are experiencing.

Unfortunately, the PFC has big limitations in terms of its processing capacity and uses a lot of resources to get there. Think of your PFC as the basket of a hot air balloon – the basket may be small, but it takes a lot of energy to fill the balloon and get it off the ground. This is why it's so easy to get distracted when you're tired or hungry – you simply don't have the fuel to keep the basket afloat, to keep your PFC 'on task'.

But it's not just about the volume of work; the *type* of work you're doing also has an impact. In his book *Thinking Fast and Slow*, Daniel Kahneman identifies two types of mental processing: System 1 ('fast') thinking, which is automatic, frequent, emotional, stereotypic, and unconscious; and System 2 ('slow') thinking, which is effortful, infrequent, logical, calculating, and conscious.

System 1 thinking covers things like reading text on a sign or driving your car on an empty road – things that take little conscious effort or thought. System 2 thinking comes into play when we do things like determine the appropriateness of a particular behaviour in a social setting, or compare the price/quality ratio of two phones.

Because System 2 thinking is more mentally taxing, it chews up metabolic resources (the fuel in your blood) much faster than automatic, System 1 tasks. This means we can only do our best thinking for a limited amount of time – so when it comes to time spent working, more is not always better.

Our best-quality thinking only lasts for a limited amount of time, so prioritising needs to take priority.

It's important to understand that your capacity for quality thinking is limited. Treat it as such by allocating it to something important – prioritising.

Not only do you need to prioritise, you need to prioritise prioritising. Why? Because prioritising is itself hard work and takes a lot of PFC energy. When we prioritise, we need to bring together experiences we haven't yet had and create pictures we have yet to see as we imagine and play with future-based concepts. Unfortunately, as shown in Daniel Gilbert's book *Stumbling on Happiness*, humans are terrible at assessing how they will feel in the future – what Gilbert calls 'affective forecasting'. We forecast based on how we feel today rather than objectively assessing how our mental state is likely to look in future.

Prioritising needs to be done when we are fresh and have the mental energy to do it well.

If mental energy is our most precious resource, we need to get smart about how we use it. In his book *Your Brain at Work*, Dr David Rock suggests these three strategies:

1. Get out of your head

Write things down so that they don't have to be 'held' in your pre-frontal cortex (PFC), using up valuable energy and processing capacity.

2. Be a blocker

Do like activities together – for example, all creative writing tasks at the start of the day – and mix up the type of thinking you're doing throughout the day. Use some activities as 'recovery' for your PFC from deep complex thinking, just as you would take breaks when doing physical training. These could be things like routine, 'boring' tasks or socially-based activities.

3. Let things slide

Be clear about what *not* to prioritise. As we explored in the *Break the Negative, Build the Positive* ROBUST principle, knowing what is not useful to you frees up energy to focus on what is. Understanding when *not* to think is important. Be disciplined about not paying attention to non-urgent tasks until you have to. A useful tool for this is Stephen Covey's Urgent/Important Matrix (also known as the Eisenhower Matrix). And don't waste mental energy on tasks when you don't have all the information – deal with them once you do.

Whilst it may feel counterintuitive, we get more done, in less time, at a higher level of quality, and in a more sustainable way when we rest, refuel, and replenish our mental energy regularly. This is because we are designed to move between spending and renewing energy. The key to becoming antifragile might be found in embracing the slumps in your day – those moments when your productivity begins to ebb – and using them more intentionally to rest, refuel, and replenish, and thereby to ultimately sustain your energy for the journey ahead.

ANTIFRAGILE ENERGY

Leadering is not easy work. It takes time, effort, and energy. As I'm sure you're experiencing, leaders are being asked to do more in less time and with fewer resources than ever before. It's draining, to say the least! All the dials are moving in the wrong direction, the 'more with less' gap is getting bigger, and we are trying to stretch ourselves to bridge it. I know. I see it in my clients and I've experienced it myself.

So whilst the need for effective, high-quality performance in workplaces is increasing, the tried and tested method of putting in longer hours can't work indefinitely because time is a limited resource. This is why we need to focus on managing our energy rather than our time in order to be well and do well, because energy is a *renewable* resource. And it's a worthwhile investment.

Positive energy influences you and the people in your life in a range of ways. Studies have found that when our energy levels feel higher, we get more done in less time, our minds are sharper, our interactions with others are better, we have better health and fewer days of missed work, we feel more positive, and we persist amid daily challenges without burning out. For example, Tom Rath, author of *Eat, Move, Sleep* and one of the world's leading researchers on workplace wellbeing, found that on days when our energy levels are higher, we also experience higher levels of engagement and wellbeing and that this spills over to doing more for the people we care about, both inside and outside of work.

The Antifragile Energy Gauge

Let's check in to see how you're doing with your Antifragile Energy.

Make a note of how much you agree or disagree with the statements below using the following scale:

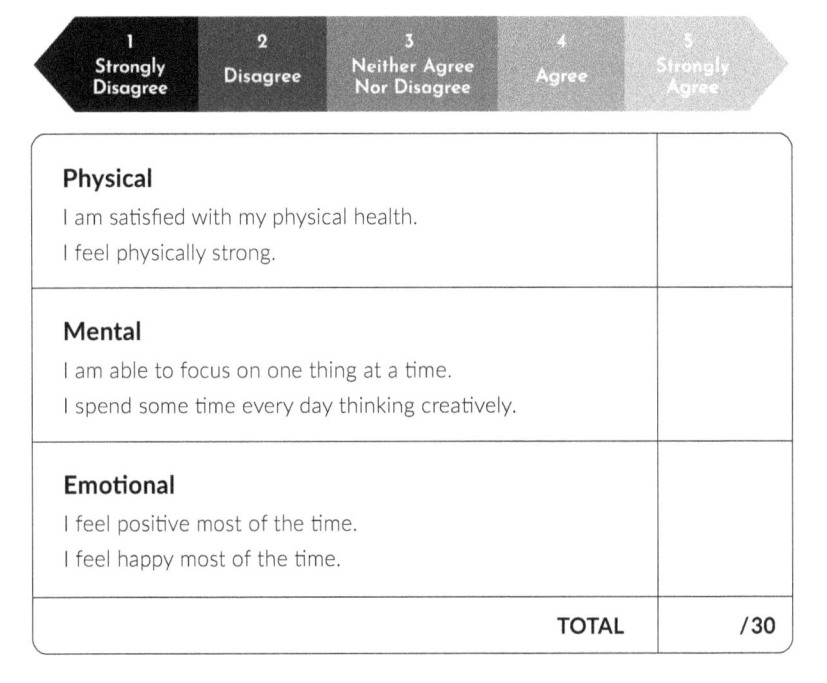

1 Strongly Disagree	2 Disagree	3 Neither Agree Nor Disagree	4 Agree	5 Strongly Agree

Physical I am satisfied with my physical health. I feel physically strong.	
Mental I am able to focus on one thing at a time. I spend some time every day thinking creatively.	
Emotional I feel positive most of the time. I feel happy most of the time.	
TOTAL	/30

The higher your score, the more Antifragile Energy you have.

As you consider your results, ask yourself:

- What's my 'energy profile' across physical, mental, and emotional energy?
- Where are the opportunities to increase and sustain my energy through different sources?
- Which of the small actions suggested in this chapter will I use to begin to renew and recharge my Antifragile Energy?

Strategies to develop your Antifragile Energy

Physical	Emotional	Mental
Make smart food choices.	Check in on your positive and negative emotional dials.	Get out of your head by writing things down.
Create space to rest.	Prioritise positivity to generate energy.	Block your day into like activities.
Become passively active.	Look for your 'jolts of joy' to build your positivity tool kit.	De-prioritise -— what don't you need to do?

SUMMARY

» Managing our energy rather than our time is key to becoming antifragile.

» Time is a finite resource; we can't create more. Therefore we need to find ways to create more sustainable and renewable personal energy sources instead.

» The three main sources of personal energy are:
- Physical
- Mental
- Emotional

» Physical energy can be increased through good food choices, consistent rest, and regular activity.

» Mental energy can be generated by prioritising, focusing, and avoiding the multitasking trap.

» Emotional energy involves prioritising positivity, whilst acknowledging the value of negative emotions as useful information. It's all in the balance!

REFERENCES

Research has found that most of us are struggling to maintain our energy levels on a daily basis ... Rath, T. (2013). *Eat, Move, Sleep: How Small Choices Lead to Big Changes.* New York, NY: Missionday, LLC

Research suggests about 95 percent of us need somewhere between seven and nine hours of sleep per night, with a few of us needing a little more or less... Jones, M. (2011, April 15) How little sleep can you get away with? https://www.nytimes.com/2011/04/17/magazine/mag-17Sleep-t.html

some studies have found that losing ninety minutes of sleep can reduce daytime alertness... Rath, T. (2013). *Eat, Move, Sleep: How Small Choices Lead to Big Changes.* New York, NY: Missionday, LLC

Studies have found, however, that consistency choosing to eat wisely... Rath, T. (2013). *Eat, Move, Sleep: How Small Choices Lead to Big Changes.* New York, NY: Missionday, LLC

Did you know that physical activity... Basso, J. C., & Suzuki, W. A. (2017). The effects of acute exercise on mood, cognition, neurophysiology, and neurochemical pathways: A review. *Brain Plast. 2*(2): 127–152. doi:10.3233/BPL-160040

taking regular breaks has been found to improve both creativity and productivity... Rath, T. (2013). Eat, Move, Sleep: How Small Choices Lead to Big Changes. New York, NY: Missionday, LLC

Positive emotions have been found to produce success in life as much as they reflect it... Lyubomirsky, S., King, L., & Diener, E. (2005). The benefits of frequent positive affect: Does happiness lead to success? *Psychological Bulletin, 131*(6), 803.

Research has found that experiencing positive emotions... Fredrickson, B. L. (2013). Positive emotions broaden and build. In E. Ashby Plane & P. G. Devine (Eds). *Advances in Experimental Social Psychology* (Vol.47, pp. 1–53). Burlington VT: Academic Press.

when you're in a positive mood this expands to about 75% – an increase of over 400%!... Wadlinger, H. A., & Isaacowitz, D. M. (2006). Positive mood broadens visual attention to positive stimuli. *Motivation and Emotion, 30*(1), 87–99. https://doi.org/10.1007/s11031-006-9021-1

In 2014, social networking company The Draugiem Group... https://desktime.com/blog/17-52-ratio-most-productive-people/

on days when our energy levels are higher, we also experience higher levels of engagement and wellbeing... Rath, T. (2013). Eat, Move, Sleep: How Small Choices Lead to Big Changes. New York, NY: Missionday, LLC

THE BEDTIME ROUTINE

It was 1 am, and Charlie was exhausted. It was a month since the 'test and learn' business strategy had gone live, and the time, effort, and energy pouring into it were really taking their toll. There hadn't been more than six hours' sleep any night for the past two weeks, and regular exercise was a distant memory – not even walking! To top it all off, takeaway food had been creeping in as a regular feature of the family menu plan.

Charlie was feeling fragile, and knew it. Life was an emotional roller coaster – wonderful highs when the new ideas landed well with clients, then complete overwhelm at the prospect of delivering them. Guilt at spending so much time away from the kids – not just physically, but emotionally and mentally. And sympathy for Alex, too, who was having a tough time at work.

Despite the longer hours Charlie had been putting in, the work kept piling up, and the range of tasks was a challenge. *Oh no!* thought Charlie climbing into bed, *I forgot to call the tax office!* Adding this to the mental 'to do' list for tomorrow, Charlie knew sleep was not going to come quickly tonight...

WHAT DO YOU SEE?

- Imagine you are Charlie, and complete the Antifragile Energy Gauge. What's your score?
- How could Charlie start to replenish personal energy? What one action would you recommend?
- What's the one thing that would make the *most* difference to your personal energy?

6.

COURAGEOUS ANTIFRAGILE ATTITUDES

THERE ARE CERTAIN MOMENTS IN LIFE THAT DEFINE US AS LEADERS. These 'sliding door' moments, once we step through, take us on a new path from which there is no going back. They're often crucial experiences that test us in some way, impacting our self-belief, self-concept, and self-confidence, as well as our evolution as a leader.

Stephanie, a coaching client of mine, shared with me a story that happened shortly after she was promoted to a leadership role within the intensive care unit of a hospital. A member of her nursing team ran into her office saying, 'Dr Thomas is yelling at Vanessa [a nurse] in front of a patient!'

Pushing down mounting feelings of anxiety, Steph hurried to the patient's room, sized up the situation, grabbed Vanessa's arm, and drew her out of the room immediately. 'I'm sorry, Dr Thomas,' she said, 'but I need to speak with Vanessa in my office straight away.' Astounded, the doctor followed.

Once they were in her office with the door closed, the doctor turned on Steph angrily, saying, 'How dare you interfere with patient care?!' Steph replied, 'I'm sorry for interrupting, Dr Thomas, but in future if you feel it's necessary to shout at Vanessa, I'd be happy to vacate my office so you can do so in private. Your patient is dependent on Vanessa and my

> *What we choose to do in moments that shake us – how we evaluate the opportunity or risk that's presented to us – is fundamentally influenced by our attitudes.*

team, and you may have just damaged his confidence in her and them, which is not in your patient's best interests.' He glared, turned on his heel, and left.

Poor Steph was shaking! She sat down before her knees could cave in and took a deep breath.

Our inner Judge Judy

Attitudes are powerful but invisible forces that shape our thoughts, feelings, and actions every day – and much of the time we're not even aware of them. As Allen Klein once said, 'Your attitude is like a box of crayons that colour your world.'

Psychologists define attitudes as a learned tendency to evaluate specific objects, people, issues, or events in a particular way. So effectively, attitudes are our inner 'Judge Judy', passing down a 'ruling' on our experiences in the world. Sometimes these evaluations can be very clear – black or white, positive or negative (think Brussels sprouts or Donald Trump – you probably know what your personal 'inner ruling' is on either of them!). But they can also be mixed, leaving you unsure about an issue or person. Attitudes are often the result of experience, learning, or social norms such as upbringing and culture, and whilst they can be enduring, attitudes are also open to change.

As a leader, your attitudes have a powerful impact on your own performance and those of the people you lead. Leadership guru John C. Maxwell suggests that 'People hear your words, but they feel your attitude.' On a personal level, your attitudes impact your resilience, self-belief, and confidence; and in terms of your team, your attitudes as a leader influence their motivation, engagement, and performance. The challenge lies in the fact that we're not always aware of when or how our attitudes are at play.

Research suggests that certain attitudes correlate strongly with overall leadership effectiveness. These include having the confidence to disagree with peers and bosses; being motivated to take risks that will make a difference and create value; and connecting with others in a way that creates powerful, positive influence.

Some attitudes are easier to adjust than others, so before we start considering the attitudes that can help us become antifragile, it's useful to understand what influences how 'strong' an attitude is – because the stronger an attitude is, the more likely we will behave in alignment with it.

Attitudes are stronger when:

1. They are the result of personal experience
2. We consider ourselves an expert on the subject
3. We expect a favourable outcome
4. They are repeatedly expressed
5. We have 'skin in the game' – that is, we stand to win or lose something.

This raises some interesting questions for us as leaders as we consider the attitudes that we want to develop or adjust. At this point, it can be useful to ask yourself:

- How can I create positive personal experiences at work for myself and my team?
- How can I deepen my expertise or broaden my knowledge base to create new attitudes and diversify my thinking?
- How optimistic am I? Do I have positive expectations about the future? Do I set goals with that attitude?
- What attitudes do I bring to life through my behaviour? Do I engage in gossip and negative talk at work, or do I close down unhelpful negative talk when I hear it?

- Do I have 'skin in the game'? Am I 'invested' in a particular outcome? Is this helpful, or is it closing my perspective down?

There are three attitudes that help us become antifragile:

- Confident
- Constructive
- Courageous.

CONFIDENT

The ancient Chinese philosopher Lao Tzu, writing about leadership in his troubled times, observed that 'confidence is [a person's] greatest friend'. And in the Decade of Disruption, this is just as true today.

Studies suggest that there is a statistically significant association between leadership effectiveness and confidence. Leaders with higher self-confidence are rated significantly more positively by their teams, peers, and bosses on a number of leadership traits, including having the courage to challenge standard approaches and lead change, being a champion for innovation, having the enthusiasm and energy to inspire others, supporting the 'tribe' internally, and representing the tribe effectively with external groups.

None of this happens by accident.

To be a confident and effective leader, we need to do things on purpose – we need to take intentional action.

There's a big difference between *having intentions* and *leading intentionally*. We all have daily intentions – what we *plan* to do, what we *could* do. Some intentions are little, like whether you'll stick to your healthy eating plan and choose salad for lunch, and some are big, like whether you'll take that new job offer.

In contrast, *leading intentionally* requires purposeful action. The good intentions you hold in your head are meaningless without the action to bring them to life. When your positive intent is put into action in the world, then you are *leading intentionally*.

The challenge is that sometimes it's easier to just go with the flow.

I'm sure that you've experienced a meeting run by a less-than-intentional leader. I know I have! You know the ones – no agenda, fuzzy actions, loose timelines, no agreed accountability, people leaving the meeting before it ends… It's a pet hate of mine, because I have a thing about respecting people's time and I'm left wondering, *Why did I bother showing up if no one else cares?*

Intentional leaders focus on creating meaningful progress by doing work that only they can do and empowering others to do the same.

It can be easy to slip into less-than-intentional leadership, particularly as we become increasingly time-poor through competing commitments, meetings, special projects, and travel. Any of these can derail the good intentions we, as good leaders, might have.

Judy Nelson, author of *Intentional Leadership: Using Strategy in Everything You Do and Say*, suggests that an intentional leader's every action is deliberate and designed to secure a particular outcome. I believe it goes even further than this.

Why 'meaningful progress'?

Research by Teresa Amabile and Steven Kramer explored what makes employees enthusiastic about work. They spoke with 600 managers across various industries and analysed nearly 12,000 diary entries provided by 238 employees from 7 companies.

The results?

Five influencing factors make employees enthusiastic about work:

1. Recognition for good work (this was top for managers)
2. Incentives and rewards
3. Interpersonal support
4. Clear targets and goals
5. A clear sense of progress (this was top for employees).

'Hang on,' I hear you say, 'aren't progress and performance just different ways of saying the same thing?'

Not exactly, no. Let's take a closer look at why.

Progress involves development over time or advancement through a series of events or milestones. On the other hand, **performance** is the act of performing; it is centred around achievement and accomplishment. This distinction between progress and performance speaks to the ROBUST principle *Tackle the Infinite Game*. It also connects with Carol Dweck's work on growth and fixed mindsets, which we introduced in the principle *Take Intelligent Risk*. You may remember that a fixed mindset focuses on achieving outcomes over learning, while a growth mindset focuses on personal improvement *through* learning, with achievements occurring as a by-product. We'll come back to this in more detail when we talk about Antifragile Mindsets in the next chapter.

When we become intentional about focusing on learning goals to create progress, we generate a different attitude – in ourselves and in the people we lead.

What happens when we become intentional about learning goals?

Sometimes fortune smiles on us, and we do well even when there is no intention behind the goal. Unfortunately, this *accidental performance*

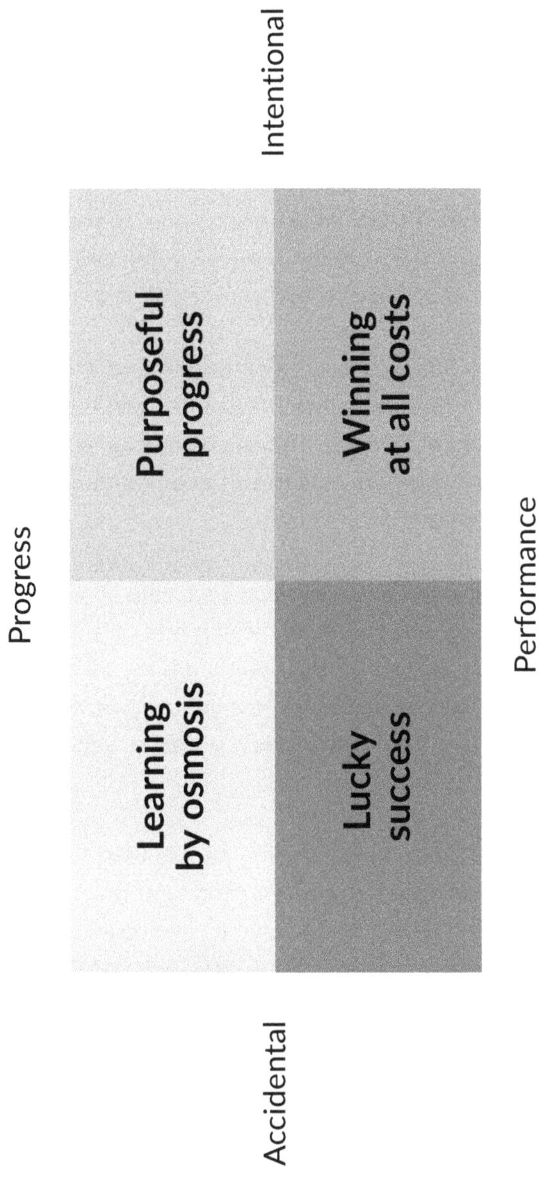

COURAGEOUS ANTIFRAGILE ATTITUDES

	Intentional	
Progress	Purposeful progress	Winning at all costs
	Learning by osmosis	Lucky success
	Accidental	Performance

Figure 6.1: The purposeful progress matrix

involves very little learning, so replicating that success in the future is hard. This kind of 'one-hit wonder' is what I call **lucky success**.

At other times, we are fortunate enough to learn simply by being in a certain environment. This is **learning by osmosis**. For example, imagine being posted to an established high-performing team and learning from the way they function. In this situation, you will make *accidental progress*. It wasn't something you were aiming to do, so you may not get as much learning out of the experience as you potentially could. However, you will still be able to draw on that knowledge and learning in future.

When we are *intentionally* aiming for *performance*, our eyes are on the prize – KPIs, goals, outcome measures – and this can create an attitude of **winning at all costs**. This can be damaging to relationships and integrity, as achieving outcomes becomes the prime driver of motivation and action.

When we aim for *intentional progress*, we create an environment that focuses on moving us closer to achieving mid- and long-term goals through learning. Because of this, learning is meaningful and, importantly, replicable, which means progress gains momentum and is easier to make in the future. This is **purposeful progress**, and it is the ultimate aim.

Being intentional doesn't mean telling people what to do, nor does it mean ruthless adherence to a plan. As confident, intentional leaders we balance the natural tension between the need to focus on a plan and the need to be flexible in its execution. We *Seek Collective Wisdom* by encouraging discussion among teams and creating space in meetings for the plan to evolve. We empower people to speak up, to make decisions, and to do the work they need to do to make purposeful progress. We are clear about deadlines, owners, and accountability – and we make this information public to create a culture of follow-through and intentionality.

How to develop a confident, intentional attitude

1. Consider your past successes and identify the personal strengths that underlie your high performance – the root causes of your success. How can you intentionally use them to contribute to making progress?

2. Take credit where it's due. If we continually explain away good performance through other people's efforts, we diminish our own confidence. How can you 'own' your efforts and achievements and help others do the same?

3. Use social comparison to motivate, not decimate. Seeing people who we believe are like us (in terms of their personal characteristics and general experience) achieve their goals through effort and persistence can be a powerful source of aspiration and motivation. How can you learn from others' qualities and experiences to grow and improve?

CONSTRUCTIVE

One of our key responsibilities as leaders is to spur action in others through a positive vision of what can be achieved – a realistic, hope-filled vision that inspires and motivates us and the people we lead to stay the course, ride the ups and downs, and be our best.

Apollo 13 is one of my favourite movies of hope. You may find that surprising, but Ed Harris' character – Gene Kranz, the NASA Flight Director in charge of the moon mission – gives a great example of how leaders can use a hope-filled vision to uncover and leverage strengths and realise performance potential at both the individual and the team level.

In case you don't know the story, Kranz and his team are faced with a potentially tragic disaster when the moon mission is derailed by an internal explosion aboard the ship. It's critical moments like these that call for inspirational leadership. Kranz steps into this 'sliding door' moment by delivering a crystal-clear, laser-focused message – fuelled by hope – of what's needed:

'Gentlemen, at this moment, I want you all to forget the flight plan. From this moment on, we are improvising a new mission: How do we get our people home?

'We've never lost an American in space and we're sure as hell not gonna lose one on my watch! Failure is not an option! … I believe this is gonna be our finest hour.'

Through his attitude, which he brings to life intentionally through his words, Kranz calms his team, provides clear direction, and instils confidence in their ability to resolve the crisis. His attitude provides an optimistic and hopeful vision of the future and motivates the team to constructive action by focusing on their strengths and fuelling their confidence. Hope, optimism, and strengths – these are the essential ingredients of a constructive attitude.

Hope – the will and the way to move forward

Hope lifts the human spirit and helps us persevere in the face of challenge. Hope sees the positive future we can achieve if we keep moving forward, adjusting and adapting as needed.

> *A hopeful leader sees beyond today's challenges to tomorrow's solutions.*

Research suggests that whilst 89% of us believe the future will be better than the present, only 50% believe that we can make it so. In a world that is increasingly challenging and complex, hope and optimism are often seen as soft, unrealistic, and pointless. However, in the world of science, hope and optimism are far more tangible, and are recognised as essential leadership qualities in the Decade of Disruption.

A leader with an optimistic attitude has positive expectations about the future, and research suggests that this has a real and significant

> *If leaders can't imagine a positive vision for themselves and their team, how can they expect their people to progress towards a better future?*

impact. As we covered in the *Build the Positive* ROBUST principle, optimistic attitudes influence how we approach problems and challenges, and our capacity to cope successfully with adversity. This is because positive future expectations lead an optimistic leader to set more challenging stretch goals and to deal with setbacks as temporary roadblocks rather than complete derailers. They expect things to work out in the end and take action to make that happen. A leader with a pessimistic attitude, on the other hand, is more inclined to give up in the face of adversity. After all, they expected things to go badly right from the beginning.

Where we see the impact of optimism really take off is when it is paired with a good dose of hope.

The Merriam-Webster dictionary defines hope as 'desire accompanied by expectation of or belief in fulfillment', but in psychology the definition is far more specific. Professor Rick Snyder, who developed Hope Theory and led much of the research in the field, defines hope as 'the process of thinking about one's goals, along with the motivation to move toward those goals (agency), and the ways to achieve those goals (pathways).'

Hope, according to Snyder's model, involves three elements:

1. Identifying 'want to' – as opposed to 'have to' – goals. This is called 'goal thinking' and it defines where you're hoping to go.
2. Developing specific pathways to reach those goals and make your hopes a reality. Scientists call this 'pathways thinking', but we can think of it simply as 'waypower'. What's the way forward to reach your goals?
3. Generating and sustaining the motivation to use these pathways to fulfil your hopes. Scientists call this 'agency thinking', but we

can think of it as willpower. How are you going to maintain the will to make your way possible and achieve your goals?

HOPE = Goal thinking + Willpower + Waypower

Figure 6.2: The hope equation

Snyder and his colleagues found that hope not only lifts your spirits, it also buoys your energy, makes life seem worthwhile, and changes your day-to-day behaviour. Hope brings together your head, your heart, and your hands as your rational and emotional selves combine to guide your actions.

What does hope look like in action?

People with high hope support their goals with **regular, committed action** and creatively think of **different strategies** for working towards them. They understand that disappointments and **challenges are a natural part of life** and so **persist** in the face of these challenges. Overall, they have a **growth mindset**.

Researchers have found that hope plays a central role in driving persistence, motivation, goal setting, and innovation. In fact, a meta-analysis has found that, all other things being equal, hope leads to a 14% increase in productivity by making people feel more engaged and enthusiastic about work. That equates to about an hour a day for most of us. Now that's worth investing in!

Importantly for us as leaders, hope also generates relational energy because people with high hope are interested not only in their own goals, but also in the goals of others. They are also able to take the perspective of others, and perceive themselves to have more social support, more social competence, and less loneliness. Win-win-win!

So, goal thinking – knowing where you want to go – is the starting point for hope. When we pair optimism with hope, our goal thinking is more expansive. We set more challenging, 'moonshot' goals, because

Leaders with hopeful, optimistic attitudes that amplify strengths produce a potent cocktail of positive energy that generates and sustains progress and high performance.

we expect things to go well. When we then consider possible pathways (waypower) and our levels of personal agency (willpower) for the goal, we prevent our optimism from going too far and becoming 'Pollyanna-ish'; we keep it pragmatic and grounded in reality. This is the realistic optimism we covered in the ROBUST principles.

There is one more ingredient to add to our constructive Antifragile Attitude to really give it a kick: strengths.

Taking a strengths-based attitude means that we evaluate things – ourselves, other people, processes, projects – by looking first and foremost for inherent strengths and opportunities for improvement and development.

As we explored in the *Build the Positive* ROBUST principle, people who understand and use their strengths report many positive outcomes, including lower levels of depression, higher levels of vitality, and good mental health. From a leader perspective, studies have found that leaders who focus on the strengths of their team members benefit from lower staff turnover, higher productivity, more satisfied customers, and greater profitability.

So as you can see, there's a lot to be said for adopting a strengths-based attitude. When we incorporate this into our constructive attitude blend, we engage the waypower of hope and intentionally look for pathways that allow us to use our strengths. In doing so, we harness the energy, engagement, and satisfaction that powers the high performance associated with strengths, and harness the inherent motivation that comes with it – our willpower – along the way.

How to develop a constructive attitude

1. Set optimistic, 'want to' goals.
2. Identify multiple pathways to achieve the goal and identify what you need to *do* and *deliver* to make progress.
3. Ask a strengths-based question in every meeting for a week.

COURAGEOUS

Are you courageous? Are you a courageous leader? What does that even mean?

I used to berate myself for not being brave enough. I wouldn't argue my point in a meeting. I wouldn't stand up for someone else, even if I could see they weren't being given the 'voice' they needed. And on the other side of the courage coin, I wasn't brave enough to admit when I was stuck, or tired, or just at the end of my tether and in need of help. I couldn't risk being vulnerable. And so I didn't ask for help, and nor did I expect others to. I can see now that I didn't have the courage to show up as being imperfect – I didn't understand that we are all in fact 'perfectly imperfect'.

Letting go of judgement and embracing imperfection can be hard. Talking about it can be even harder! So what do these kinds of conversations look like?

A courageous attitude lets go of judgement, accepts the perfectly imperfect nature of yourself and others, and embraces the risk and vulnerability that comes with that.

Sometimes, it means you're naming the 'elephant in the room' – the thing that no one is talking about, but everyone knows is there. At other times, you're challenging the status quo, the 'legacy practices' that have been around for so long that they're part of the cultural fabric of your family, your team or organisation. Or it can be personal – the one-on-one conversation with a colleague or a team member about their performance that asks us as leaders to step into our courage and have 'skin in the game' in the conversation.

When we have these conversations, it means we care enough to get uncomfortable – within ourselves and in our relationships with others – so that we can be honest and address what's not working well enough. For these conversations to be effective, we must be willing to suspend judgement, to be generous and curious, and to take the risk of feeling vulnerable by really talking and really listening, from the heart as well as the head. The challenge is that when we do this, it can feel like we're risking our relationships and personal status. As we touched on in the *Seek Collective Wisdom* ROBUST principle, social connectedness and standing are primary human needs, so when we put these on the line it can feel very unsafe.

The other problem is that many of us simply don't know *how* to have these difficult conversations. When you pair that with a sense of personal risk triggering the safety switch in our brains, it's not surprising that we avoid it – just as I used to. But the reality is that it's far more effective for us to speak up so that we can learn and move forward as a group, rather than let it fester. And in the case of the one-on-one conversation, it's kinder to speak up than to bite your tongue or keep 'fixing' things yourself, because when you do this you deny the other person the opportunity for learning and growth.

Adopting a courageous attitude means having conversations that act as sliding door moments in our relationships by building trust, connection, and psychological safety. Professor Brené Brown suggests that you're ready to do this when:

- You're ready to sit next to someone rather than across from them.

- You're willing to put the problem squarely in front of you, rather than in front of another person or between you and them.

- You're ready to listen, ask questions, and accept that you may not fully understand the issue.

- You recognise other people's strengths and understand how they can use them to address their challenges.
- You can hold someone accountable without shaming or blaming.
- You can model the vulnerability and openness you expect to see from others.

How to develop a courageous attitude

1. Cultivate curiosity and suspend judgement by asking questions rather than making statements. Give yourself a target ratio of questions to statements (e.g. 1:1, one question for every one statement) and look to increase the ratio over time (e.g. 3:1).

2. Stretch your comfort zone for speaking 'against the flow'. My youngest daughter is an expert at this 'oppositional conversational style': she just disagrees with whatever anyone says! If you're not ready to go to that level yet, start by just asking a question to encourage more discussion around the issue.

3. Have a kind coaching conversation. If you truly respect and value someone, then the kind thing to do is talk with them clearly and directly about what is not working. You can do this by asking them:
    - How do you feel things are going?
    - What's working well from your perspective?
    - Where do you feel like you're struggling?
    - What can we learn from this experience?
    - What support do you need?

ANTIFRAGILE ATTITUDES

In any workplace, engaged and disengaged employees work side by side. The one thing that differentiates them is their attitudes to their work. As leaders, our attitudes have a powerful impact on our own performance and that of the people we lead – both formally and informally, and in our professional and our personal lives. Positive attitudes help us become antifragile because they influence personal resources such as self-belief and confidence, which helps us engage with disruption, challenge, and change more effectively.

By tuning into your attitudes and becoming more conscious and aware, you will be able to question and ultimately stop the self-limiting and self-sabotaging thoughts, feelings, and behaviours that stem from unhelpful and out-of-date attitudes. Developing Antifragile Attitudes will help you get moving, identify and take the right action, and build momentum to create the positive change and impact that you want in your life and in your leadership.

The Antifragile Attitudes Gauge

Let's check in to see how you're doing with your Antifragile Attitudes.

Make a note of how much you agree or disagree with the statements below using the following scale:

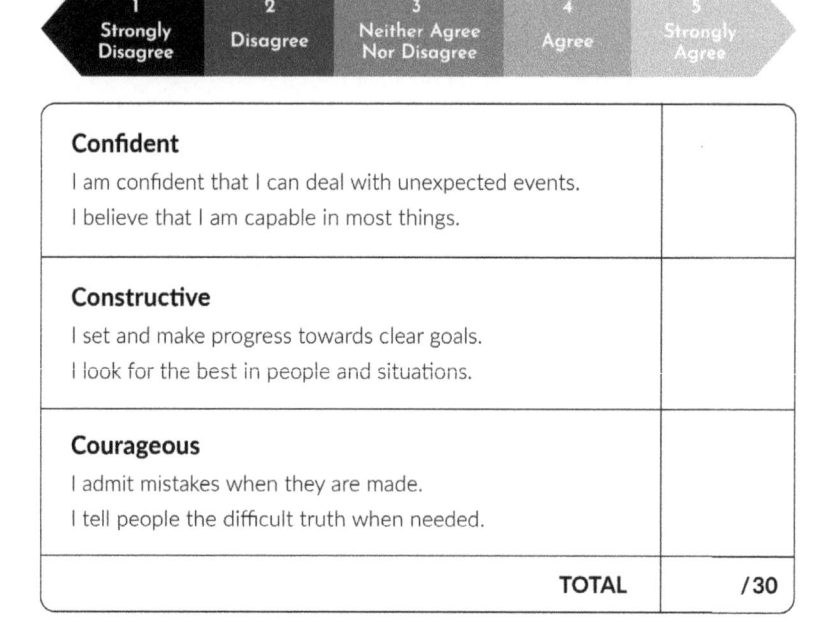

| 1 Strongly Disagree | 2 Disagree | 3 Neither Agree Nor Disagree | 4 Agree | 5 Strongly Agree |

Confident I am confident that I can deal with unexpected events. I believe that I am capable in most things.	
Constructive I set and make progress towards clear goals. I look for the best in people and situations.	
Courageous I admit mistakes when they are made. I tell people the difficult truth when needed.	
TOTAL	/30

Your overall AntiFragile Attitude score is out of 30

The higher your score, the more Antifragile Attitudes you have.

As you consider your results, ask yourself:

- What's my 'attitude profile'?
- Where are the opportunities to develop Antifragile Attitudes?
- Which of the small actions suggested in this chapter will I use to begin my 'attitude adjustment' efforts?

Strategies to develop your Antifragile Attitudes

Confident	Constructive	Courageous
Identify root causes of your past successes.	Set 'want to' goals.	Cultivate curiosity by asking more questions.
Take credit where it´s due.	Identify multiple pathways to achieve goals and what you need to do and deliver to make progress.	Engage in 'oppositional conversational style'.
Use social comparison to motivate, not decimate.	Ask appreciative questions.	Have a kind coaching conversation.

SUMMARY

» *Attitudes are powerful but invisible forces that shape our thoughts, feelings, and actions. They are so ingrained by our society, family, and culture that most of the time we're not even aware of them.*

» *The three attitudes that help us become antifragile are:*
- *Confident*
- *Constructive*
- *Courageous.*

» *A confident attitude is cultivated by being intentional about how best to contribute to making purposeful progress.*

» *A constructive attitude involves hope, optimism, and looking for strengths.*

» *A courageous attitude emerges when we embrace vulnerability, suspend judgement, and stay curious to have kind conversations that support growth and accountability.*

REFERENCES

Psychologists define attitude as a learned tendency to evaluate specific objects, people, issues, or events in a particular way... Williams, P., Kern, M. L., & Waters, L. (2017). The role and reprocessing of attitudes in fostering employee work happiness: an intervention study. *Frontiers in psychology, 8*: 28.

Research suggests that certain attitudes correlate strongly with overall leadership effectiveness... https://www.forbes.com/sites/joefolkman/2016/02/03/5-attitudes-that-define-great-leaders/#6b70941bf99d

Studies suggest that there is a statistically significant association between leadership effectiveness and confidence... https://www.forbes.com/sites/joefolkman/2019/02/12/how-self-confidence-can-help-or-hurt-leaders/#3a4cc11e5990

Research by Teresa Amabile and Steven Kramer... Inner Work Life: Understanding the Subtext of Business Performance. *Harvard Business Review*, May 2007 https://hbr.org/2007/05/inner-work-life-understanding-the-subtext-of- business-performance.

Carol Dweck's work on growth and fixed mindsets... www.mindsets.com

A leader with an optimistic attitude has positive expectations about the future... Arakawa, D., & Greenberg, M. (2007). Optimistic managers and their influence on productivity and employee engagement in a technology organisation: Implications for coaching psychologists. *Int Coaching Psych Rev. 2*(1):78–89.

Research suggests that whilst 89% of us believe the future will be better than the present, only 50% believe that we can make it so... Lopez, S. J. (2013). *Making Hope Happen: Create the Future you Want for Yourself and Others.* New York, NY: Simon and Schuster.

Snyder and his colleagues found that hope not only lifts your spirits... Snyder, C. R. (2003). *Psychology of Hope: You Can Get There from Here.* New York: Free Press.

hope leads to a 14% increase in productivity by making people feel more engaged and enthusiastic about work... Reichard, R. J., Avey, J. B., Lopez, S., & Dollwet, M., (2013). Having the will and finding the way: A review and meta-analysis of hope at work. *The Journal of Positive Psychology, 8*:4, 292–304. doi: 10.1080/17439760.2013.800903

**Studies have found that people who understand and use their strengths report many positive outcomes, including lower levels of depression, higher levels of

vitality, and good mental health... McQuaid, M., & Lawn, E. (2014). *Your Strengths Blueprint: How to be Engaged, Energized and Happy at Work.* Albert Park: VIC. Michelle McQuaid P/L

From a leader perspective, studies have found that leaders who focus on the strengths of their team members... (Corporate Leadership Council, 2004; Hodges, & Asplund, 2010; Clifton & Harter, 2003; Harter, Schmidt, & Hayes, 2002; Lavy & Littman-Ovadia, 2016)

Professor Brené Brown suggests that you're ready to do this when... Brown, B. (2018). *Dare to Lead: Brave Work. Tough Conversations. Whole Hearts.* UK: Random House.

A CONFERENCE CALL WITH SAM

Alex took a deep breath as Darcy, the Assistant Project Manager, left the room. In five minutes, Alex had a conference call with Sam, one of the longest-standing members of the team. Sam had worked on a project with this client before and had strong and established relationships in the organisation. Unfortunately, this time around Sam was causing issues in the team.

Darcy had just told Alex that he'd heard directly from the client that Sam was talking about other team members (including Alex) in an unprofessional way. Darcy was worried it was undermining the team's credibility, and Alex had to agree. Darcy had also spent some of the last 20 minutes sharing how, in addition to being unprofessional, Sam hadn't delivered the data that was needed for the client update that afternoon. Alex was annoyed with Sam for compromising the team's ability to meet the client's expectations and wondered if it was deliberate. There were rumours that Sam had expected to be leading this project and had been less than pleased at being 'passed over' in favour of Alex.

Alex knew that this was a critical conversation to get things back on track with the client and the team, but the preparation time Alex had planned for the call was now gone, and with it any confidence that the meeting was going to go well. What was it that Glenn had said at the lunchtime 'grilling' last week? *Failing to plan is planning to fail.* Well, that seemed to be just where this meeting was heading. With an all-too-familiar knot of anxiety, Alex clicked open the conferencing link to see Sam looking cool, calm, and confident in the conference room of the US office.

WHAT DO YOU SEE?

- Based on the situation outlined above, what words would you use to describe Alex's attitude?

- Which of the Antifragile Attitude strategies do you think would be most useful to Alex in this conversation with Sam?

- If you had to have this conversation with Sam, how would you approach it?

7.

INFINITE ANTIFRAGILE MINDSETS

INVESTMENT FIRM BLACKROCK IS A NEW YORK STOCK EXCHANGE–listed investment company with an annual revenue of nearly 4 billion USD and an asset management portfolio of nearly 7 trillion USD (as at 2019). Because of its sheer size, *The Economist* once referred to BlackRock as the world's largest 'shadow bank'.

In January each year, BlackRock CEO Larry Fink writes a letter to inves- tors. This highly regarded letter influences conversations inside boardrooms around the globe. In 2020, it addressed the finance industry's role in important environmental and social issues such as climate change. By all accounts, it represents a significant shift in the way mainstream finance firms are starting to think about their role in shaping the relationship between climate change, business, and investment.

The letter explained that BlackRock would avoid investments in companies with a high sustainability-related risk. It would also opt out of investments in coal production, introduce funds that ban fossil-fuel stocks, and vote against corporate managers who aren't making progress on fighting the climate crisis. It suggested that the world is moving inexorably in the direction of investing in companies that are actively working to address climate change or at least do no harm, and that investors who ignore this pendulum swing do so at their peril.

Let me share with you a few key paragraphs from the letter:

> Dear CEO,
>
> As an asset manager, BlackRock invests on behalf of others, and I am writing to you as an advisor and fiduciary to these clients. The money we manage is not our own. It belongs to people in dozens of countries trying to finance long-term goals like retirement. And we have a deep responsibility to these institutions and individuals – who are shareholders in your company and thousands of others – to promote long-term value.
>
> …
>
> While government must lead the way in this transition, companies and investors also have a meaningful role to play. As part of this responsibility, BlackRock was a founding member of the Task Force on Climate-related Financial Disclosures (TCFD). We are a signatory to the UN's Principles for Responsible Investment, and we signed the Vatican's 2019 statement advocating carbon pricing regimes, which we believe are essential to combating climate change.
>
> …
>
> The importance of serving stakeholders and embracing purpose is becoming increasingly central to the way that companies understand their role in society. As I have written in past letters, **a company cannot achieve long-term profits without embracing purpose and considering the needs of a broad range of stakeholders.** A pharmaceutical company that hikes prices ruthlessly, a mining company that shortchanges safety, a bank that fails to respect its clients – these companies may maximise returns in the short term. But, as we have seen again and again, these actions that damage society will catch up with a company and destroy shareholder value. By contrast, a strong sense of purpose and a commitment to stakeholders helps a company connect more deeply to its customers and adjust to the changing demands of society. **Ultimately, purpose is the engine of long-term profitability.**

> …
>
> We believe that when a company is not effectively addressing a material issue, its directors should be held accountable. Last year BlackRock voted against or withheld votes from 4,800 directors at 2,700 different companies. Where we feel companies and boards are not producing effective sustainability disclosures or implementing frameworks for managing these issues, we will hold board members accountable. **Given the groundwork we have already laid engaging on disclosure, and the growing investment risks surrounding sustainability, we will be increasingly disposed to vote against management and board directors when companies are not making sufficient progress on sustainability-related disclosures and the business practices and plans underlying them.**

Fink's letter shows Antifragile Mindsets in action. At the foundation of his approach is a commitment to contribute to the greater good in the long term, with the understanding that what is good for people and the planet can also be good for the purse strings. Inherent in this is acceptance that disruption and change are a natural part of growth and development. These commitments to the greater good of people and planet are then made personal by asking, *What is my part in this? How can I contribute? Where does my personal responsibility lie?* Fink's answers to these questions lay in the direction he has chosen to take BlackRock.

Fink's letter demonstrates three key Antifragile Mindsets:

- Growth
- 'ReflActive' (no, this is not a typo – all will become clear soon!)
- Benefit.

Later in the chapter, we'll look at what each of these mindsets is about and why they are so critical for leaders. But first things first – what's the big deal about mindsets?

MINDSETS 101

Nothing you do happens by accident. Every choice you make is the result of your thoughts, your feelings, and, finally, your actions. Whether you're ordering coffee, choosing where to live, or anything in between, your mindset is always 'on'.

But have you ever wondered *why* you do certain things or think in the way you do?

It all comes down to your mindsets: the sets of beliefs you hold about how the world works. But just because your mindsets are established doesn't mean they're set in stone. Mindsets can be changed.

A mindset is a lens or frame of mind through which you view the world.

Mindsets help you make sense of the world by simplifying and organising the plethora of information you need to process in any given moment. In every area of your life, including work and relationships, you are operating from a certain mindset. Mindsets aren't just a reflection of your reality – they actually interact with and shape your life.

For example, in one research study, a group of hotel housemaids were taken through a training workshop in which they were encouraged to see their work as 'good exercise' rather than 'just work'. After four weeks, despite no change in their behaviours or routine outside of work, the maids had experienced changes in objective measures, including reductions in both weight and blood pressure. They also reported improvements in subjective measures such as body image and job satisfaction. The control group – housemaids in the same hotel who did not participate in the training workshop – experienced none of these benefits.

Mindsets interact with your reality, shaping it in self-fulfilling ways as they tip off a cascade of psychological and physiological effects.

The only thing that changed for these maids was the way they *viewed* the incidental exercise they undertook while working.

They changed their mindset, and the physiological changes in weight and blood pressure suggest that their body followed suit. Such is the power of mindset.

There is growing evidence that our mindsets affect outcomes in many domains of life, including:

- **Intelligence** – our intelligence is boosted when we believe we can work towards being smarter, as opposed to just being born with a certain level of intelligence
- **Ageing** – positive beliefs about getting older can impart both physiological and psychological benefits
- **Response to stress** – the way we perceive stress can moderate its psychological and physiological effects
- **Willpower** – our beliefs about our levels of willpower impact how much we stick at things when faced with challenge.

In the Decade of Disruption, stress is a particularly relevant example, so let's take a closer look at how our 'stress mindset' can impact our capacity to deal with it.

Your stress mindset is the extent to which you believe that stress can have *enhancing* consequences – a 'stress-is-enhancing mindset' – or *debilitating* consequences – a 'stress-is-debilitating mindset' – for performance and productivity, health and wellbeing, and learning and growth.

Research by Alia Crum and colleagues at Stanford University suggests that mindset significantly shapes the stress response, as well as perceived health and life satisfaction. Following exposure to an acutely stressful situation, those participants who self-reported having a stress-is-enhancing mindset experienced more moderate cortisol reactivity (physiological response) and were more receptive to feedback (behavioural response) than those with a stress-is-debilitating mindset. Crum's research also suggests that we can change our stress mindset in order to improve how we feel about our health and work performance.

> *Changing your mindset about stress can meaningfully influence your body's stress response.*

Importantly, having a stress-is-enhancing mindset doesn't mean you must see all stressful situations as good. Rather, it is about noticing opportunities for learning and growth within the inherent struggle of challenging situations. So rather than being an exercise in positive thinking, this mindset is about being open to the *possibility* that stress can be good for you. Taking this more balanced view will help you fear stress less, cope with it better, and use it as a resource to learn, grow, and engage with life on a whole new level.

Building mindset awareness

Becoming aware of your mindsets means getting curious about what your beliefs and expectations are and tuning in to your 'internal radio' (as mentioned in the section on mental energy). You will have noticed that we are talking about mindsets, plural: you will have different mindsets in different areas of your life.

Here are a few questions to help you develop awareness around your mindsets and understand how they may be feeding unhelpful unconscious biases.

Do you believe people are inherently good or bad?

Leaders who believe that people can be inherently bad may, perhaps unconsciously, lack trust in others' motivations and behaviours. They see people as a problem to be solved rather than a capacity and opportunity to be realised.

Do you believe intelligence is fixed, or developable?

Leaders with an 'intelligence is fixed' mindset have a more fragile sense of confidence in their ability, are less likely to take on stretch goals, and tend to avoid feedback.

Do you believe that conflict is positive, or negative?

Leaders with a reflective mindset are able to appreciate a diverse range of opinions that may be very different from their own. They recognise that, when managed effectively, conflict and difference in opinion can add value to discussions and promote better outcomes.

As you tune into your mindsets, always remember to ask yourself the key question:

There are three mindsets that help us become antifragile, and they are the same three we identified earlier for BlackRock CEO Larry Fink. They are:

- Growth
- ReflActive
- Benefit.

Let's take a look at each in turn.

GROWTH MINDSET

How your mindset can hold you back

Tony was an up-and-coming Marketing Executive for a client of mine – a large. fast-moving consumer goods company. He was convinced that he would never be good at public speaking. He struggled with leading even small meetings, and it was holding him back from progressing in his career. We began to work together, and I recorded his journey. When I showed him the footage just six weeks later, he was blown away by the improvement he had made. He couldn't understand why he hadn't tried before. But I knew why. The problem was simple: his *mindset* had gotten in the way.

Do you, too, believe that you cannot change? Do you see your abilities as so static that change is simply impossible, and there's no point in even trying? If so, you have a *fixed mindset*.

As we touched on in Chapter 3, if you have a fixed mindset, you believe that things don't, won't, and can't change, including your skills and knowledge. If, on the other hand, you have a *growth mindset*, you believe that your personal qualities and situation are open to change and can be developed throughout life. The beliefs underpinning the growth mindset have now been borne out by science. Advances in neuroscience and fMRI (functional magnetic resonance imaging) technology have confirmed that our brains can indeed continue to build new neural pathways – the building blocks of learning – right up until the day we die. This capacity for change is called *neuroplasticity*.

Carol Dweck's research suggests that when you have a fixed mindset, you aim for less challenging goals; you are less likely to seek or heed feedback; and you have a lower opinion of your own ability – and this holds true across a wide range of ages. It was also found that people with a fixed mindset were more open to cheating in tests because they were desperate to retain their (fixed) status as 'smart' and couldn't face the possibility of failure.

Of particular relevance to our leadering is the impact of a fixed versus growth mindset on the types of goals we set for ourselves and others. Because people with a fixed mindset place higher value on *looking* smart (as opposed to learning and *becoming* smarter), they tend to set performance goals that they are confident they can achieve, rather than stretch goals that prioritise learning new skills and move us towards mastery.

Performance goals are about 'winning positive judgments of your competence and avoiding negative ones'. When people pursue performance goals, they are doing so because they want to look smart – to themselves or others – and avoid looking dumb. This usually leads them to 'play it safe'.

Learning goals are about increasing competence. In Dweck's words, these goals reflect 'a desire to learn new skills, master new tasks, or understand new things – a desire to get smarter.'

Both types of goal can drive achievement; however, overall the evidence suggests that focusing too much on performance rather than learning outcomes leads to a fragile sense of competence, reduced perseverance and resilience, and reluctance to take on developmental feedback.

A focus on performance goals over learning goals makes us fragile.

You may remember from Chapter 3 that we should not make the mistake of thinking of a growth mindset as 'good' and a fixed mindset as 'bad', and that instead we should ask ourselves the one question that matters: *Is my mindset helping or holding me back in this situation at this time?*

When coaching yourself or others towards a growth mindset, it is useful to understand that the beliefs of a fixed mindset are based in fear. Having a fixed mindset is ultimately about our brains wanting to feel safe which, as we covered in the *Recruit the Brain* ROBUST principle, is its primary function. So a good general approach when seeking to shift a fixed mindset is to consider how you can increase feelings of safety and security. After all, building trust in ourselves and others helps to create psychological safety, which drives innovation and helps us become antifragile.

Dial up your growth mindset through a learning narrative

As we discussed in the ROBUST principle *Operate in Reality*, we humans try to make sense of the world by creating stories that we tell ourselves about what's happening now and what might happen next. Over time, the stories we tell ourselves can become more embedded and act as the basis for our mindsets – the relatively stable, often unconscious assumptions we make about ourselves, other people, and the world around us. But as we know, these stories are not always accurate. And this is a big deal because, as we covered earlier, the mindsets they create have a powerful influence over how we feel and behave.

Cognitive behavioural therapy (CBT) helps people recognise 'triggers' in their lives, tune into the unhelpful stories that they tell themselves in times of stress, and then challenge them by creating alternative stories that support more helpful feelings and behaviours. The aim of CBT is not to eliminate negative or upsetting emotions, but rather to develop healthy, realistic thoughts that enable us to respond to situations in an appropriate and healthy way.

So, where possible, try to apply the concepts of CBT in your own life. Tune in to your inner dialogue – your internal radio – and when you hear a fixed mindset song, gently challenge it. Shift your internal dialogue from an inner critic to a kind and wise friend.

For example:

> *When you hear: 'I'm rubbish at…'*
> Gently challenge it with: 'I can become better through effort and practice.'
>
> *When you hear: 'There's no point in trying if I'm going to fail'*
> Gently challenge it with: 'It's just an experiment; if it does fail, I can learn, reassess, and do something different next time.'
>
> *When you hear: 'I'm not surprised they gave me negative feedback, I know they never liked me'*
> Gently challenge it with: 'It's not about me personally. Where is the nugget of learning in this for me?'
>
> *When you hear: 'I've always been told I'm no good at…'*
> Gently challenge it with: 'No one can know my potential. I must discover it for myself.'

REFLACTIVE MINDSET

A client of mine, Sheena, received an internal promotion to Financial Director for a global health brand. As she moved into this new role, we worked together to establish her brand, presence, and voice within the Executive Team. After we'd been discussing a recent 'critical meeting' with her global counterparts, she told me how much she had gained from reflecting on the meeting. She talked about the new insights, different perspectives, new ideas, and new strategies we'd created together for her to improve for next time.

Reflecting on our experiences is a valuable source of learning. The literature recognises reflection as a key behaviour for leaders who want to develop themselves and move up the leadership ranks.

Unfortunately, when we think back over our experiences, we can fall into the trap of **rumination**: stewing over a problem or experience. This unhelpful habit has been shown to deplete mental and emotional energy and is even correlated with depression. In contrast, when we **reflect**, we evaluate our actions, decisions, mistakes, and successes in a constructive way that enables learning.

Reflective learning allows leaders to quickly get up to speed in new situations; to deal with unfamiliar circumstances by recognising connections with seemingly unrelated situations; to question their assumptions; and to make better decisions by learning from experience – to avoid making the same mistake twice! You can see how a growth mindset and a reflective mindset support and sustain each other through their learning focus.

Moving from reflection to reflAction

Reflection is usually done retrospectively – you have an experience, *then* you think about what happened and how you performed. However, scholar and researcher Donald Schön suggests that reflection is most effective when it relates closely to real-time action and experience.

> *Reflection enables us to take a step back, to get 'up on the balcony' to systematically review past events through an impersonal, strategic lens with the goal of learning and improvement.*

This proactive approach to reflection is the essence of the reflActive leader mindset.

Schön makes the distinction between reflection and reflAction by defining reflection as 'reflection *on* action', i.e. after the event, and reflAction as 'reflection *in* action', i.e. conscious thinking and modification in the moment. The reflActive leader thinks *in parallel* with their actions. They are open and curious about what is happening and reflect on the action *whilst* experiencing it.

ReflAction is also sometimes referred to as meta-thinking, meta-cognition, or meta-consciousness. The experience of observing yourself in the moment is a critical element of mindfulness, which mindfulness expert Jon Kabat-Zinn describes as 'paying attention … on purpose, in the present moment and non-judgmentally.' Being mindful helps us get up on the balcony *whilst in the moment* and gives us more information from which to draw insights afterwards.

Neuroscientist David Rock, in his book *Your Brain at Work*, uses the metaphor of the 'Director' to explain what happens in our brains when we step outside and observe our moment-to-moment experience. He suggests that with practice, we can make decisions about how our brain responds to situations and – like a director – sometimes even alter the script.

Live in the Learning Loop

The reflActive mindset encourages growing and learning from experience, both good and bad. This real-time learning means engaging the 'Director' in your brain more often. That might seem hard to do when there's a lot going on or when you feel under pressure, but if our brains are 'primed' with a recent experience of engaging the Director, it becomes much easier. So we need to find a simple way to activate the Director often – a method that we can build into our everyday life.

We can do this by engaging our Tinkering skills to move through the Learning Loop we introduced in the ROBUST principle *Use Intelligent Risk* – to Act, Assess, and Adjust.

In order to *Recruit the Brain* and build its capacities, we must repeat the Learning Loop over and over to reinforce those neural pathways and move towards mastery. Living in the Learning Loop widens our perspective on problems, broadens our knowledge, and develops our skills. It keeps us focused on playing the game rather than winning it, and encourages us to reflect on our behaviour in order to acquire new insights that can help us develop more effective leadership strategies for dealing with disruption, challenge, and change.

BENEFIT MINDSET

As a leader with a growth mindset, you understand that development is possible throughout your life. You believe that it is not inherent ability or talent but effort, perseverance, and a willingness to learn from mistakes that breed success. As a leader with a reflActive mindset, you are intentionally curious and open to learning from experience. You reflect in real time on your thoughts, actions, and behaviours, and assess their impact on yourself and others.

A benefit mindset takes this one step further…

What lies beyond a growth mindset?

This was the question Ash Buchanan, a Master of Applied Positive Psychology student at The University of Melbourne, asked a few years ago whilst I was teaching Applications of Positive Psychology.

Ash is a deep, thorough systems thinker and the quality of his work on mindsets is excellent. Ash suggested that a limitation of Carol Dweck's work on fixed versus growth mindset is that it disconnects learning and accomplishment from the broader context of leadership and purpose.

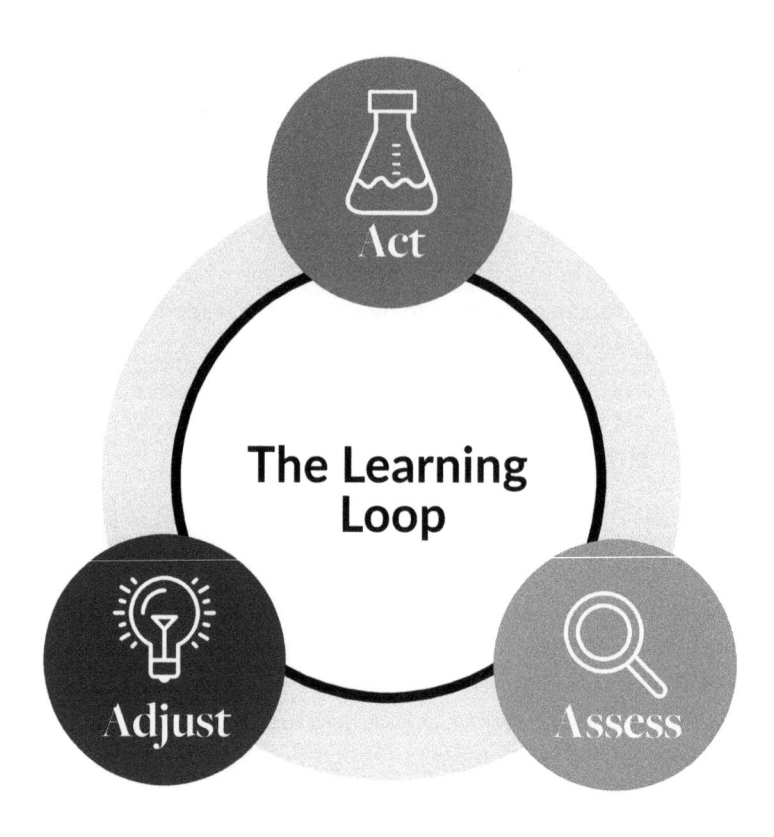

Figure 7.1: The Learning Loop

With that in mind, Ash applied himself to developing the idea of a benefit mindset. In conjunction with co-author Dr Peggy Kern, Ash describes the benefit mindset thus:

The Benefit Mindset describes everyday leaders who discover their strengths to make valuable contributions to causes that are greater than the self, leaders who believe in making a meaningful difference, positioning their actions within a purposeful context.

We can think of mindsets as existing on a continuum. A growth mindset encourages us to think about *what* we do, and a reflActive mindset asks us to consider *how* we do it at an individual level. A *benefit* mindset moves beyond the individual level to consider the collective. It moves beyond what we do and how we do it to consider a greater question: *why?*

Never has there been a more crucial time for us to fully appreciate and consider the interwoven nature of human and ecological flourishing.

The benefit mindset positions individual development and effort within a collective, purposeful context and offers a way for us to consider what it means to learn *and* lead – to achieve *and* collectively contribute. It focuses on how leaders can not only thrive individually, but create the context and conditions for others to thrive as well. The benefit mindset is based in the understanding that our ability to flourish as individuals is fundamentally connected with the communities and systems to which we belong. It is the mindset of participants in the infinite game.

Fostering a benefit mindset

The first step in developing a benefit mindset is simply to ask yourself: *What's my legacy? How does my leadership impact other people?* Look beyond the short term to consider what your leadership might mean on a longer timeframe and broader horizon. Now ask yourself: *What do I want my legacy to be? How can I change my behaviour to have a more positive impact in my community and the world at large?*

Fixed MINDSET	**Growth** MINDSET	**Benefit** MINDSET
Everyday experts who seek perfection and avoid failure	**Everyday learners** who seek growth and development	**Everyday leaders** who seek to 'be well' and 'do good'
Focus on reproducing **what** they know	Focus on improving **how** they do what they do	Focus purposefully on **why** they do what they do
Believe their strengths are innate gifts that can't be developed and focus on **perfecting their abilities**	Believe their strengths can be developed with effort, reaching **higher levels of achievement** and ability	Believe in developing their strengths and **meaningfully contribute** to a future of greater possibility

Figure 7.2: Comparing fixed, growth, and benefit mindsets Source: Buchanan & Kern, 2017

ANTIFRAGILE MINDSETS

As we've seen, mindsets are far more than just a reflection of reality. They are the lens through which we see the world, and they shape the story we tell ourselves to make sense of it. But while mindsets can be immensely helpful, they also have a dark side. By creating expectations of the way the world 'should' be, they can be a powerful source of unconscious bias.

By definition, we are unaware of unconscious beliefs – so it's easy to act as if they don't exist. But the reality is that our unconscious mind influences our actions just as powerfully as our conscious mind, if not more. So often we believe we are acting in line with our conscious intentions, when really our unconscious is in the driver's seat. When there is a gap between our unconscious expectations (our 'should be's) and our conscious reality, we feel pain and discomfort. So it makes sense to become more in tune with, and work towards changing, our unconscious biases. In this way, we can 'close the gap'.

By developing Antifragile Mindsets, we become more open to growth and learning in the pursuit of meaningful long-term goals, and this equips us to cope – or better still, thrive – in the face of disruption, complexity, and the unexpected.

THE ANTIFRAGILE MINDSETS GAUGE

Let's check in to see how you're doing with your Antifragile Mindsets.

Make a note of how much you agree or disagree with the statements below using the following scale:

| 1 Strongly Disagree | 2 Disagree | 3 Neither Agree Nor Disagree | 4 Agree | 5 Strongly Agree |

Growth I experiment with new ideas and new ways of doing things. I take on challenges that come my way.	
ReflActive I frequently take time to think about the impact of my behaviours on others I regularly seek feedback about my work.	
Benefit The work I do is important to other people. The things I do contribute to society.	
TOTAL	/30

Your overall AntiFragile Mindset score is out of 30

The higher your score, the more Antifragile Mindsets you have.

As you consider your results, ask yourself:

- What is my 'mindset profile'?
- Where are the opportunities to develop Antifragile Mindsets?
- Which of the small actions suggested in this chapter will I use to begin growing my Antifragile Mindsets?

Strategies to develop your Antifragile Mindsets

Growth	ReflActive	Benefit
Set learning goals.	Cultivate mindful awareness.	Use your talents and strengths for the greater good.
Challenge your fixed mindset and silence your inner critic.	Consciously move through the Learning Loop in real time.	Identify your legacy.

SUMMARY

» Our mindsets help us make sense of the world; they are the lenses through which we process everything we experience.

» Mindsets can be changed with focused and consistent effort.

» There are three mindsets that help us become antifragile:
- Growth
- ReflActive
- Benefit

» We cultivate a **growth mindset** by focusing on learning goals rather than performance goals and shifting our internal dialogue from an inner critic to a kind and wise friend.

» We develop a **reflActive mindset** by cultivating mindful awareness of our thoughts and actions in real time and moving through the Learning Loop often so that we can be agile and adapt.

» With a **benefit mindset** we play the infinite game, move beyond the individual to the collective, and consider not just what we do and how, but why.

REFERENCES

The Economist once referred to BlackRock as the world's largest 'shadow bank'... https://www.economist.com/special-report/2014/05/08/shadow-and-substance

In one study a group of hotel housemaids were taken through a training workshop in which they were encouraged to see their work as 'good exercise' rather than 'just work'... Crum, A. J., & Langer, E. J. (2007). Mind-set matters: exercise and the placebo effect. J Psychol Sci. 18(2): 165–71.

Intelligence - whether we believe we can work towards being smarter or if we are just born that way... Dweck, C. (2006) *Mindset: The New Psychology of Success*. New York, NY: Random House.

Ageing – whether our positive beliefs about getting older have beneficial physiological/psychological outcomes... Levy, B. R., & Myers, L. M. (2004). Preventive health behaviors influenced by self-perceptions of aging. *Preventive Medicine*, 39(3): 625–629.

Response to stress – whether stress can have a positive impact on us... Crum, A. J., Salovey, P., & Achor, S. (2013). Rethinking stress: The role of mindsets in determining the stress response. *Journal of Personality and Social Psychology*, 104(4): 716–733.

Performance goals... Learning goals... Dweck, C. S., & Leggett, E. L. (1988). A social-cognitive approach to motivation and personality. *Psychological Review*, 95(2): 256.

The literature recognises reflection as a key behaviour for leaders who want to develop themselves and move up the leadership ranks... https://hbr.org/2018/09/how-self-reflection-can-help-leaders-stay-motivated

This unhelpful habit has been shown to deplete mental and emotional energy a... McLaughlin, K. A., Borkovec, T. D., & Sibrava, N. J. (2007). The effects of worry and rumination on affect states and cognitive activity. *Behavior Therapy*, 38(1): 23-28. https://doi.org/10.1016/j.beth.2006.03.003.

Schon makes the distinction between... Schön, D. A. (1983). *The Reflective Practitioner: How Professionals Think in Action*. New York: Basic Books.

The Benefit Mindset describes... Buchanan, A., & Kern, M. L. (2017). The benefit mindset: The psychology of contribution and everyday leadership. *International Journal of Wellbeing*, 7(1), 1–11.

A PROJECT-CRITICAL PRESENTATION

Alex and Charlie flopped onto the couch, both sighing heavily. 'The kids' bedtime routine feels like it keeps on taking longer and longer, doesn't it?' said Alex, glancing at the clock.

'Yep,' Charlie replied, 'it's past 10 pm and I've still got at least three hours' work I could do. Not sure I've got the energy, to be honest! How about you – anything you need to do for tomorrow?'

'I've got a client presentation at 10 am,' Alex said in a voice that betrayed a deep sense of dread. 'I *hate* presenting; I've never been any good at it and never will be. Not like Sam – always so smooth and clear – and funny! I mean, who's relaxed enough to be funny when they're presenting? Not me, that's for sure. I've got to get approval for additional funding, and I'm really worried that the client's taking calls from our competitors. If I lose this project, that's it – my career is over.'

This was a familiar scenario. Charlie recognised Alex's usual response to a 'project critical' presentation. 'Hey, come on, you've done it before and got through just fine – what did you do before that you can do again tomorrow? Have you had any feedback from Glenn?' Charlie cajoled.

Alex shrugged. 'I don't know – she mentioned a few things after the last one, but I think she was just annoyed with me because I added a couple of extra slides to the deck without checking with her. I tried to work on it today, but Darcy was in my office again telling me how dreadful things are with the project and the team – and Sam! Guess I'd better go and get started on it. See you in bed… at some point before sun-up I hope!' With yet another big sigh, Alex got up from the couch.

WHAT DO YOU SEE?

- If Alex had approached the situation with an Antifragile Mindset, how might it have played out differently?

- How do you think Alex is feeling in terms of physical, mental, and emotional energy in this current mindset?

- Which of the three Antifragile Mindsets do you think would be of most help to Alex right now?

PART IV

FROM BECOMING TO BEING

Right. Off you go then! You've got your map, travel guide, and personalised route plan. Nothing can stop you now! Or can it?

If getting started is hard, keeping going can be even harder. So in this section we'll explore how moving from becoming to being antifragile can help. We'll also look at what the latest research on behaviour change can tell us about creating helpful habits to keep you moving forward on your journey.

It doesn't happen by accident or osmosis. Becoming antifragile takes effort, energy, and intention. Fortunately, neuroscience, psychology, and behavioural science are teaching us more and more about how to create effective change in human mindsets, attitudes, and behaviours. We are beginning to understand why good intentions are not enough, and why motivation only takes us so far. We are learning more about how the brain responds to change and what we can do to nudge it in the right direction. We are realising that our brains are wired to connect with others, and that social support, context, and environment play a critical role in enabling us to learn, develop, and change. We can use all of this in our journey to becoming antifragile.

But at some point, we need to transition from taking steps towards becoming antifragile to actually *being* antifragile. This is the difference between *playing* the violin and *being* a violinist; the difference between someone who is 'on a diet' and someone who eats healthily. It transitions from being part of your behaviour to part of your identity. Antifragility is not something you *do,* it is *who you are*. It shines through in your beliefs; in the way you interpret the world; in how you think, feel, and behave; and ultimately in how you show up for yourself and others.

So how can we move from Becoming to Being?

8.

ANTIFRAGILE IDENTITY

SO HERE YOU ARE, READY TO TAKE YOUR FIRST STEPS ON THE Becoming Antifragile journey. Do you feel ready? I hope so. I hope that you feel you know antifragile pretty well by now. You've scoped the landscape, opened the map, and located your position on it. You've dived into the ROBUST principles of the Becoming Antifragile Travel Guide and explored what your personal route planner could look like through the lenses of Antifragile Energy, Antifragile Attitudes, and Antifragile Mindsets. But that's not to say it won't still feel a little intimidating! So let's see how we can make those first steps a bit easier to take…

Are you familiar with the Hero's Journey?

It's a classic story structure in which a character sets out on an adventure to achieve a goal. They face uncertainty and conflict, experience challenge and growth, and ultimately triumph over adversity. Coined by academic Joseph Campbell in 1949, the Hero's Journey structure is recognisable in stories throughout time, from *Jason and the Golden Fleece* to *Finding Nemo*, *The Lion King*, and *Star Wars*. It is so common and ingrained in books, films, television, and Netflix dramas that it's become part of our cultural DNA.

In case you're not familiar with it, broadly speaking, the Hero's Journey takes place in three stages:

The Departure – leaving the 'ordinary world' and venturing into unknown territory (the 'special world').

The Initiation – experiencing 'rebirth' through various trials and challenges.

The Return – returning transformed and triumphant.

You may think the Becoming Antifragile journey is like this. But let's be clear: it isn't! And there are three main reasons why:

1. You don't have to leave the 'ordinary world', because that's exactly where the disruption, challenge, and change is happening. The Becoming Antifragile journey takes place in the real world – your living room, your office, your team meeting, your family – right here, right now, day in, day out.

2. There is no 'rebirthing', because that assumes you have no need for the you that came before. In becoming antifragile we *Use Intelligent Risk* gained through previous experiences to Tinker, so that we improve through the uncertainty and challenges of the journey.

3. There is no 'triumphant return' because that suggests the journey is over. The Becoming Antifragile journey doesn't end, because in the Decade of Disruption the world is never simple, stable, or predictable for long. There is always new 'unknown territory', which makes the Becoming Antifragile journey an infinite game.

Becoming antifragile involves personal disruption, challenge, and change.

However, the two journeys do have one important element in common – experiencing trials and challenges by venturing into unknown territory. It is likely that becoming antifragile will demand different things of you and your leading; it will ask you to see the world differently, to loosen and perhaps let go of some of your deeply held beliefs, and to show up and behave in a different way. There's no doubt that becoming antifragile will involve personal disruption, challenge, and change.

GOING DEEPER

The work of Donella Meadows identified that there are multiple places to intervene in order to create change, each with varying levels of effectiveness. Ironically, the quickest and easiest ways to intervene are often the least effective in achieving change outcomes. For example, public health campaigns often focus on outcomes that are readily and easily measured (such as the number of incoming calls received to a help line) rather than addressing the deeper question - and more potent leverage point - of why the change is important and the impact it will have in the future.

My PhD research looked at how we create change for wellbeing in organisations, and as part of that research I developed and tested a model proposing that change is more successful when it addresses both 'inside-out' and 'outside-in' factors. What does that mean? Well, inside-out factors are an *inherent* part of the system – they can't operate independently from it. So for the system of you, these are things like your attitudes, mindsets, knowledge, skills, and behaviours. Outside-in factors, on the other hand, *influence* the system and its capacity to change, but are not part of it – they are 'outside' the system. So if we look once again at the system of you, these might be things like your boss, your team, the culture of your organisation, your social support network, your opportunities for development, and so on. These are resources you can draw on to effect change, but they are not part of who you are.

Meadows' work suggests that one of the most effective levers available to create change is a shift in mindset. And for our Becoming Antifragile journey, this means a shift in the way we see, think, and feel about ourselves. A shift in identity.

THE SIX WS

Who, What, When, Where, Why, and hoW are critical tools in journalism, research, and police investigations. They're also useful questions for us to consider when thinking about changing behaviour.

Professor B. J. Fogg, author of *Tiny Habits: The Small Changes That Change Everything* and Director of the Behavior Change Lab at Stanford University, suggests that we start with why (motivation), then progress to what, how (ability), when and where (prompt), and finally who (social support). Simon Sinek also suggests that we *Start with Why* and then move to what and how whenever we are trying to make positive change. However, James Clear, author of *Atomic Habits*, proposes that we must start with who we want to become, then think about how we're going to get there (processes) and finally what we want to achieve (outcomes).

Whilst I agree with both Fogg and Sinek in the importance of why, what, and how, when it comes to becoming antifragile, I'm with Clear: identity is *the* critical leverage point for change, and the clear (no pun intended!) starting point for becoming antifragile.

I think of becoming antifragile as a five-stage process of identifying *who* you want to be (identity), then *why* you want to be that person (motivation), *what* you want to achieve (outcomes), and *how* you are going to do it (process). And finally, what support you might need to succeed and sustain the change.

Who am I?

Your identity embodies the answer to the question *Who am I?* It includes your motivation, beliefs, and worldview, as well as your assumptions and biases. If outcomes are about *what* you achieve and processes are about *how* you get there, identity is about *who you want to become*. And this is high-octane fuel when it comes to motivation for sustained action! It moves you from 'I want to become antifragile' to 'I am *being* antifragile'. For a change in behaviour to stick, it must involve identity

ANTIFRAGILE IDENTITY

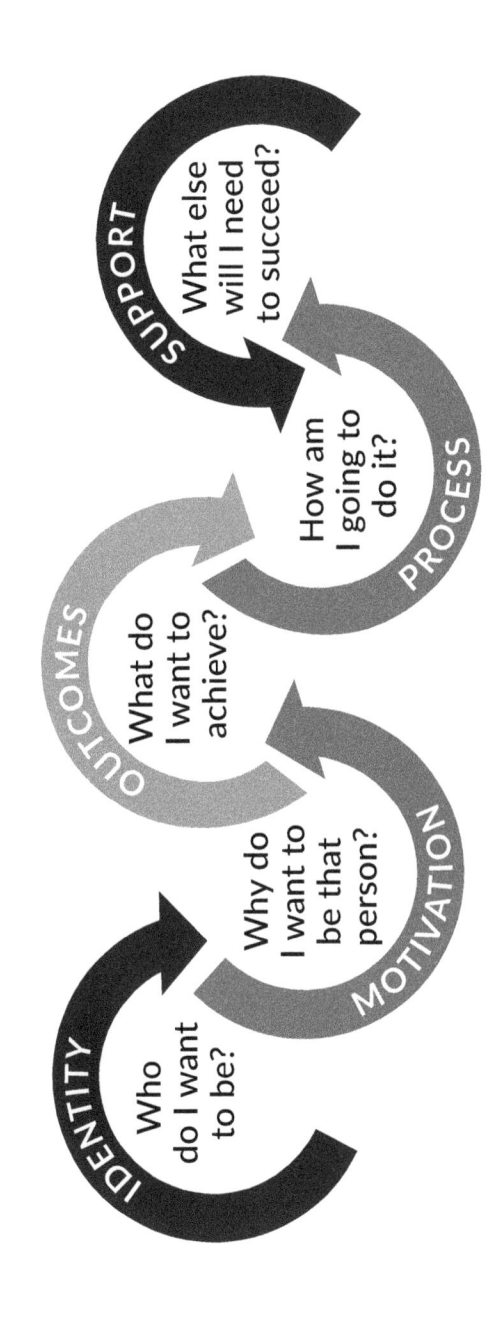

Figure 8.1: Creating your Antifragile Identity

change. Improvements will only ever be temporary until they become part of who you are.

So, the question I invite you to ask as you embark on your antifragile journey is this: Are you becoming the person you want to be? The first step is not why, what, or how, but *who*. And that's up to you. You get to choose the identity you want to reinforce through your energy, attitudes, mindsets, and behaviours; through the 1% behaviours you choose to adopt or change today. A 1% behaviour is something small enough to make a difference over time, but not big enough to create resistance or fear that may stop you starting right now. The work of neuroscientist Dr Joe Dispenza suggests that your regular patterns of behaviour (your habits) bring your identity to life – literally. They are the repeated, lived experience of your identity.

Becoming antifragile requires you to continuously edit your beliefs to upgrade and expand your identity. When your behaviours and your identity are fully aligned, you are no longer becoming antifragile – you are simply acting like the type of person you already believe yourself to be; you are *being antifragile*. This integrates action (what), process (how), and identity (who) so that you literally *become* your habits.

In every moment, you have a choice: to move towards being antifragile, and in doing so to affirm and reinforce your Antifragile Identity, or to move away from it. The five-stage process we explored earlier can help you do this, but you first need to know who you want to be. You have the power to choose and change your beliefs about yourself, and the most practical way to do this is to change what you do: your habits.

James Clear explains how to do this as a simple two-step process:

Step 1: Decide who you want to be (antifragile).

Step 2: Prove it to yourself with small wins.

Once you have your identity on board, change will happen – and stick

– more easily, because it is really hard to change thoughts or actions once they are connected with your identity (which can of course be a double-edged sword!). Doing a 1% behaviour once won't change your identity, but by repeating it over time you'll build new neural pathways, reinforce your belief, and gather evidence that you *can* be the person you wish to become. This is how meaningful change happens: we build the evidence base for our new identity one 1% behaviour at a time. By Tinkering, living in the Learning Loop, and being reflActive, we can make radical change.

NO-ONE SAID IT WAS EASY

Have you ever tried to change something about yourself or your life, and not succeeded? I know I have, many times. Research suggests that there are three factors that get in the way of the changes we want to create. The good news is that applying the ROBUST principles can help us navigate around them.

Factor 1: We don't really want to

Change doesn't really stand a chance if it doesn't feel meaningful for you, or if it is not aligned with your values. Feeling that it's something you *should* do, *have to* do, or are *expected* to do won't be enough. No matter how good the change might be for others in your life, or even for you personally, it's not until you *want* to create change that you'll start to make progress. By setting 'want to' goals, you tap into the approach motivation that we talked about in Chapter 4. Ask yourself: *What do I want to change that expresses who I want to be, rather than impresses others or meets their needs and expectations?*

You'll also find it hard to get change moving if it's in conflict with other things you care about. I've found this when I've tried to take on multiple changes at the same time – it feels like I'm getting pulled in too many directions. I waste energy on worrying that I'm not making progress on any goals rather than focusing on moving to constructive action.

Remember, our brains can only process so much information and can only undertake so much new neural construction at a time – we need to 'focus, focus, focus'.

To replenish your change energy, take a break from your expectations for a few days and then re-engage with your goals in small ways so that you can build confidence and momentum. The key is to assess and adjust (remember the Learning Loop). If the change continues to be something you want to do, rather than something you feel you should do, then try the next small action, reassess, and move forward from there.

Factor 2: We don't know how

As we covered in the ROBUST principle *Recruit the Brain*, our brains crave safety, but this can really hold us back when it comes to making change, because we feel the need to be certain about the choices we've made. *Seeking Collective Wisdom* helps us get around this by sharing the changes we're considering with others, along with any doubts or uncertainty.

Studies show that we increase our levels of commitment, improve our self-regulation, and are more likely to gain access to the knowledge, tools, and help we need by talking with other people. 'Go public' with a close friend, a family member, a trusted colleague, a coach or mentor, or a support group about the changes you want to make, and you'll fly over the 'don't know how' speed bump.

Factor 3: We don't think we can

Making a change can be a scary proposition for many of us. Memories of the disappointment of attempted changes that didn't work or were never fully realised come flooding back, along with stories of 'I'm not good enough', 'I have no willpower', or 'I could never pull that off.' We can end up feel demoralised and defeated before we even begin.

The only way you'll really fail is if you never to try to make the changes you want in the first place.

Dialling up your growth mindset can really help here. As we covered in *Use Intelligent Risk*, when we set learning goals rather than just performance goals, it helps us understand that success is about realising our potential for growth, not just achieving outcomes. Whether you fly, fail, or fall somewhere in between on your journey to becoming antifragile, you will have the upside of the learning and growth that comes from your efforts and experiences.

TAME THE CHANGE MONSTER

B. J. Fogg suggests that the core mechanisms of behaviour change are the same no matter what kind of behavioural change we are trying to create. His research shows that behavioural change happens when our **motivation** (our desire to do the behaviour), our **ability** (our capacity to do the behaviour), and a **prompt** (a cue to do the behaviour) all come together at the same moment. All three must exist for an action to be taken, but they will look different for each person and each situation.

Let's look at each of these three elements.

Maximise motivation

According to Fogg, 'When it comes to changing our behaviours, the problem is that motivation and willpower are shape-shifters by nature, which makes them unreliable.' His research shows that our willpower decreases from morning to evening, and our motivation for self-improvement disappears when we're tired.

In order to maximise motivation, Fogg recommends:

1. Start with your hopes and aspirations – your 'want to' goals.

2. Note down as many behaviours as you can that might make this a reality.

B = MAP

Behavior happens when **Motivation** & **Ability** & **Prompt**

converge at the same moment

Figure 8.2: The ingredients for behaviour change Source: B. J. Fogg, 2019

3. Map these behaviours to find the ones that you have the highest levels of motivation and ability to enact, and that will have a high impact.

These 'want to–able to' behaviours are your 'golden behaviours' – the ones you're much more likely to stick with.

Amplify ability

Fogg's research shows that we can work around the unreliability of motivation by keeping changes small and expectations low. Small changes and low expectations? Sounds a bit like the test-and-learn mentality of Tinkering, doesn't it?

So whilst one tiny action towards becoming antifragile may feel underwhelming and insignificant, it actually helps in multiple ways: it makes your brain feel safe, it stops you from getting stuck in your own internal stories and dramas about failure, and it builds the momentum you need to ramp up to bigger challenges and faster progress. Remember the 1% rule – that is, if you can improve by just 1% each day for a year, you'll be 378% better by the end of it as the improvements compound over the 12 months!

Power up your prompt

Fogg's research team also found that behaviour doesn't happen without a prompt or 'cue'. We need the 'perfect storm' of all three elements – motivation, ability, and prompt – because we only respond reliably to prompts when we are motivated and able to do so. You either notice the prompt, or you don't. And if you don't notice the prompt, or if the prompt happens at the wrong time, then the behaviour just doesn't happen. That's why a well-timed prompt is so powerful.

So what is a prompt? You may not realise it, but you have designed many prompts in your life already. Ever made a checklist? Put a post-it note on your desk or computer? Set a reminder on your phone? These are all prompts to trigger your desired behaviour.

Fogg and other behavioural science researchers suggest that an effective way to create a prompt is to anchor a new habit to an existing, established behaviour or habit. James Clear calls this 'habit stacking'. To get started, make a list of all your habits throughout a typical day – for example, getting out of bed, travelling to work, getting your morning coffee, packing up to go home, and so on. Pick one current habit that is embedded into your day and that provides a reliable, realistic anchor for the new habit you want to develop. The goal is to minimise resistance by flowing seamlessly from your current habit to your new one, so it requires as little physical and mental energy as possible.

One more thing...

We know that personal change can be hard, particularly when we're trying to navigate environmental uncertainty and the disruption and challenge that comes with it. It's like trying to do the tango whilst juggling cats!

Neuroscience tells us that it takes repetition to build new neural pathways towards mastery, and that is true. But there is an added element that can supercharge your journey to mastery: positive emotions. It turns out that celebrating success is a powerful catalyst for change, as positive emotions lay down memories in your brain that help to build your antifragile habits. What do you do when you feel like you've nailed something, when you're feeling a sense of success and accomplishment? Do you smile? Give a fist pump? Mentally pat yourself on the back?

It doesn't really matter what you do, what matters is that you do *something* to acknowledge, celebrate, and embed your new antifragile behaviour. That means immediately, joyously, and genuinely celebrating the 1% (or more!) you have just accomplished each and every time. I know, I know, it may feel a little strange at first – but your brain will *love* it as your neural reward system lights up, providing a rush of serotonin and dopamine to help reinforce that desired behaviour in the future.

After I...

Anchor
An existing routine you can anchor your new tiny habit onto, and use as a cue.

⌄

I will...

1% **B**ehavior
The new habit routine you want scaled back to be super small and easy.

⌄

Then, I'll...

Celebrate!
Something you do to create a positive feeling of reward inside yourself.

Figure 8.3: Fogg's recipe for behavioural change Source: B. J. Fogg, 2019

So, here are the four steps:

1. **Maximise motivation** by choosing a 'want to' goal
2. **Amplify ability** by mapping the impact versus effort of your action options
3. **Power up your prompt** by anchoring and stacking it to existing habits
4. **Celebrate success** to **Recruit the Brain** and keep moving forward.

Fogg and his team advocate the 'ABC' recipe to succeed and stick with behavioural change:

Troubleshooting

If your 1% behaviour isn't working, don't beat yourself up. Instead, get curious and ask: *What is making this behaviour hard to do?*

Fogg's research has found it is likely to be one of five factors:

1. Do you have enough **time** to do the behaviour?
2. Do you have enough **money** to do the behaviour?
3. Are you physically **capable** of doing the behaviour?
4. Does the behaviour require a lot of creative or mental **energy**?
5. Does the behaviour **fit** into your current routine?

Zero in on the right problem to solve, and ask: *How can I make this behaviour even easier to do?*

For more inspiration visit www.tinyhabits.com.

SUMMARY

» *Becoming antifragile involves experiencing trials and challenges by venturing into unknown territory. It requires us to make change.*

» *Identity is the critical driver for behavioural change, and habits bring our identity to life through lived experience.*

» *Habits represent and build evidence for* **who you are**, *so by changing them you can choose* **who you want to become**.

» *Considering who you want to become and why you want to be that person is the first step on the journey to becoming antifragile.*

» *Applying the ROBUST principles can help us navigate around the three factors that can get in the way of changes we want to create:*

   1. *We don't really want to*
   2. *We don't know how*
   3. *We don't think we can.*

» *Research by B. J. Fogg found that the 'formula' for behavioural change is: Behavioural Change = Motivation + Ability + Prompt (+ Celebration!)*

REFERENCES

Research suggests that there are three factors that get in the way of the changes we want to create... Prochaska, J. O., & Prochaska, J. M. (2016). *Changing to Thrive: Using the Stages of Change to Overcome the Top Threats to Your Health and Happiness.* Simon and Schuster.

Studies have found we increase our levels of commitment... Klein, H. J., Lount, R. B., Jr., Park, H. M., & Linford, B. J. (2020). When goals are known: The effects of audience relative status on goal commitment and performance. *Journal of Applied Psychology, 105*(4), 372–389. https://doi.org/10.1037/apl0000441

His research found that behavioral change happens when... Fogg, B. J., & Euchner, J. (2019). Designing for behavior change – new models and moral issues. *Research-Technology Management, 62*(5): 14–19. doi: 10.1080/08956308.2019.1638490

"When it comes to changing our behaviors, the problem is that motivation and willpower are shape-shifters by nature, which makes them unreliable,"... https://www.michellemcquaid.com/podcast/do-you-need-a-tiny-wellbeing-habit- podcast-with-bj-fogg/

The work of Donella Meadows identified that there are multiple places to intervene... Meadows, D. H. (1999). *Leverage Points: Places to Intervene in a System.* http://www.scrummaster.dk/lib/AgileLeanLibrary/People/DonellaMeadows/donellameadows.org-Leverage%20Points%20Places%20to%20Intervene%20in%20a%20System.pdf

The work of neuroscientist Dr Joe Dispenza suggests that your habits bring your identity to life... Dispenza, J. (2011). Breaking the habit of being yourself: How to lose your mind and create a new one. *Energy Psychology Journal, 3: 2: Theory, Research, and Treatment,* 57.

Your identity embodies the answer to 'Who am I'?... Myers, David G. (2009). *Social Psychology* (10th ed.). New York: McGraw-Hill Higher Education.

LEVELLING UP

'Oh, and Sam, thanks for your support in the meeting earlier today. I really appreciated you backing me up on the supply issue and I'm sure we can make this work with the new timeframes.' Alex hung up from the video call with a wry smile. Who would have thought six months ago that Sam would be such a strong support with this client? Things had certainly come a long way!

Alex paused to reflect on the conversation with Sam and what had changed over the past six months to bring them to this point. Well, there had certainly been personal change: Alex felt more confident, had more energy, and was less stressed and anxious about leading the team. With this new frame of mind it was easier to think more clearly and that had created the courage and motivation to take risks and try new ways of doing things.

What else had changed? Alex pondered. There certainly wasn't just one thing. The changes Charlie had made at home – simpler routines for the kids and a focus on eating healthily – had definitely made a difference. So had Glenn's mentoring and the executive coach she had organised. Alex now understood more about how the brain works, how it can get in the way of progress, and how having a 'closed door' policy at specific times could help make the most of mental energy.

The drama and emotional leakage 'lesson' from Glenn had been a real game changer too. She had helped Alex understand how to proactively lead the team in constructive conversations focused on progress towards project milestones, rather than wasting time on 'emotional venting'. Glenn had also encouraged Alex to get used to 'smart failing' by trying new things and seeing what worked, since she believed trial and error had been the foundation of her own leadership success.

And of course, there was *that* conversation with Sam. *I had to dig deep for that one,* Alex remembered. *But there's no doubt it was a tipping point in shifting the team dynamics and my own confidence. I had no idea what was going on for Sam outside of work. Putting the effort in to understand really gave me a different perspective and helped build a stronger, more effective relationship with him.*

Alex made a few notes on the pad on the desk in preparation for the next conversation with Sam. *What had gone well? Where did I struggle? What did I learn? What will I try next time?* These were the four questions the executive coach had suggested to use after every meeting or presentation to capture learning and keep making progress. 'Live in the Learning Loop to keep levelling up,' she'd said.

And that was exactly what Alex intended to do.

WHAT DO YOU SEE?

- Based on the excerpt above, what three words would you use to describe Alex?
- What's the biggest change you see between this Alex and the one we've been following in previous chapters?
- Given the information provided here, what's one thing Alex could do to continue the Becoming Antifragile journey?

AFTERWORD

It can be easy to read a book like this and use it to affirm our existing self-concept. I know because I've done it – often! I'll read something and think *Oh yes, well I already knew that* or *I already do that*.

My invitation to you as you reflect on what you'll take and do from reading this book is to let go of the need to affirm what you *think* you already know or already do. Instead, be curious about the ideas and questions here and consider: *How can I use that in my life? When, with whom, and for what purpose?*

As you do this, here are three principles to help guide you:

1. You are the expert of you
 No-one knows you better than you. Each journey to becoming anti-fragile is unique. Challenge yourself, stretch your boundaries, but do what makes sense to you, in your life and your context.

2. Have skin in the game
 Take meaningful action that has meaningful consequences for you. Be specific about your prompt and your action so that you know exactly when the situation or opportunity arises and can't let yourself off the hook.

3. Don't pick cherries
 Be honest in your assessment of your actions, and don't be selective with your information. Dig deep to find the truth – the whole truth!

Before we part ways and you embark on your journey, there is one overriding principle that we must cover:

> *Thou shalt not have antifragility at the*
> *expense of the fragility of others.*
> – NASSIM NICHOLAS TALEB

There is an ethical consideration to becoming antifragile, which is that we must not do so to the detriment of others. We must not make others fragile in the process of making ourselves antifragile. Optionality does not give us licence to be irresponsible in relationships or careless with people's emotions. Courageous conversations should build, not break a person's confidence and capacity for growth. Seeking diverse opinions is about empowerment, not power play. In becoming antifragile we give a helping hand and lift others up on their journey to becoming antifragile, too.

There have definitely been times where I've felt like Alex did at the start of the book – 'just getting through'. I'm sure you have too. This book was written with you, me, and Alex in mind. I hope you've discovered a range of useful ideas and actions that you can apply to your personal and professional lives every day to become antifragile. To learn to love adventure, risk, and the unknown. To leverage randomness and chaos rather than hide from them. To live, love, and grow through the unseen, the opaque, and the inexplicable. In doing so, I hope you are able to lean into uncertainty, grow through challenge and change, and learn to thrive in this Decade of Disruption.

Travel well.

HOW CAN I HELP?

It is my heartfelt hope that the ideas in this book provide you with the map, provisions for your pack, and principles you need to take with you on your journey to becoming antifragile. But if you or others in your world would like some extra guidance on the journey, I'd be delighted to help you.

Keynote speaking

If you're looking to create not just an event but an experience that empowers people to embrace uncertainty, challenge, and change with confidence and clarity, look no further.

I've helped hundreds of people leverage their leadership to become antifragile, creating positive, purposeful impact for them and the people they lead. Offering practical evidence-based strategies they can immediately apply, I leave people with the confidence and motivation to learn to thrive as they navigate uncertainty, challenge, and change.

Find out more here: www.drpaigewilliams.com/speaking

Corporate education

Want to make the most of your leadership potential and the capacity of your team?

Using a potent blend of positive psychology, neuroscience, systems thinking, my own research, and real-world leadership experience, my online and face-to-face development programs provide practical, evidence-based strategies to help people become antifragile, elevate performance and create positive, purposeful impact.

Find out more here: www.drpaigewilliams.com

Mentoring and executive coaching

I'm often asked by leaders if they can use me as a sounding board on how to deal with a specific leadership challenge. These leaders don't need a full coaching program, but could do with an injection of perspective, advice, or expertise to help their thinking. My mentoring sessions are the perfect answer.

Coaching is a powerful and effective way to leverage your leadership and level up your capacity and performance. I love working one on one with executives to craft an individualised development plan tailored to meet their personal hopes, ambitions, and learning needs.

Find out more here: www.drpaigewilliams.com

LET'S STAY IN TOUCH…

I'd love to stay connected, and I appreciate and respect that time and attention are your most precious resources.

My regular blog, *Leverage Points*, offers the latest leadership ideas, research, and evidence translated into everyday actions that will encourage an antifragile, Tinkering mindset and motivate you to try new practices in your leadership.

Occasionally, when I've got something exciting and new to share, I'll send one of my resources as a learning gift and let you know about upcoming conference presentations.

You can sign up to stay in touch here: www.drpaigewilliams.com/connect

I hope to hear from you soon!

Lightning Source UK Ltd.
Milton Keynes UK
UKHW010936150722
405904UK00001B/208